# Haoles in Hawai'i

# HAOLES IN HAWAI'I
*Race and Ethnicity in Hawai'i*

SERIES EDITOR: Paul Spickard

# HAOLES IN HAWAI'I

JUDY ROHRER

University of Hawai'i Press
Honolulu

**Library of Congress Cataloging-in-Publication Data**

Rohrer, Judy.

Haoles in Hawai'i / Judy Rohrer.

p.   cm.—(Race and ethnicity in Hawai'i)

Includes bibliographical references and index.

ISBN 978-0-8248-3405-0 (softcover : alk. paper)

1. Whites—Hawaii.   2. Race awareness—Hawaii.   3. Hawaii—Race

relations.   4. Hawaii—Colonization.   I. Title.

DU624.7.W45R64 2010

305.809'0969—dc22

2010017411

Designed by Josie Herr

Printed by The Maple-Vail Book Manufacturing Group

*For*
*Georgia K. Acevedo*
*and*
*Dorrie Mazzone,*
*the best mother-partner team*
*a girl could hope for*

# Contents

# Foreword

*Haoles in Hawai'i* is the inaugural volume in a succeeding series on ethnicity planned by the University of Hawai'i Press. Such a project is a reminder that academic presses are clusters of the energies and intelligences that help to make up and maintain a civil and literate society. Without such influences and resources our lives would all be poorer and meaner. We in Hawai'i are fortunate to have such a press.

That the press has launched this series with a volume whose title appears to make haole an ethnic identity will likely violate what most of us haoles have long assumed—that other people are ethnics, not us. The author, Dr. Judy Rohrer, compellingly sucks us in to this shock of recognition with an account of her own awakening to this social fact at age seven in rural Kaua'i. In arguing that ethnicity is a sociopolitical construct, not a genetic fact, she marches us through several centuries of Hawaiian history and such fields as colonial, gender, and whiteness studies.

She connects the emergence of the several ethnic identities in Hawai'i to the history of its colonial rule that began after the "discovery" of the islands in the late eighteenth century. Among the immediate consequences of "discovery" was the rapid depopulation of the Hawaiian Kingdom owing to the arrival of Western diseases against which native Hawaiian bodies carried no defenses. Such an invasion all but destroyed Hawaiian culture and society. Into this near void poured opportunists from other countries, chief among them Americans. Although there were some notable exceptions, in general their disdain for or ignorance of traditional Hawaiian practices provided them an easy right-of-way for the implantation of capitalist ways with land, its ownership practices, and social relationships. As a consequence, a century after their "discovery," Hawaiians had become strangers in a strange land—their land seized, their queen deposed, and a (largely) white oligarchy in control.

Needing vast numbers of fieldworkers for the plantation economy that they were creating, the white planters at the outset imported them from Asia (principally Japan and China) and, later, from Portugal and other Pacific Island cultures. Most of these workers stayed on. Within several generations their locally born children began to intermarry. In this way, the colonially shaped brew of races and cultures of the "local" people was produced. As for the whites, they became "haoles," itself a Hawaiian word that is a portmanteau of meanings, including white, but white with its particular local history.

These several decades later, color is no longer the master social code. Rohrer has set her task here as that of sorting out for us how both local and haole are now socially produced. Mixed ancestry is quite common; our means of distinguishing among us are based on the proportions of the cultures and behaviors we display both happily and unwittingly. The reach of Rohrer's scholarship and the lucidity of her prose in untangling this complex social identity are a masterful introduction to the succeeding volumes in the series.

PHYLLIS TURNBULL
*Professor Emeritus*
*University of Hawai'i Political Science Department*

# Acknowledgments

In many ways, I have been writing this book since my family moved to Hawai'i in 1974. Because of that it has been influenced by innumerable people—too many to thank by name. Please know my warmest mahalos go to all of you. The first to teach me about haole were my classmates at Kōloa Elementary School on Kaua'i. Some of those lessons were harder than others, but they are ones I frequently return to, and I thank each of you. I also thank those who befriended me at Roosevelt and Punahou High Schools. You helped teach me about local politics in the big city. The hiking club at Punahou, with Tai Crouch as advisor, deepened my appreciation of the *'āina*. My education about race relations and colonization continued during summer internships at the American Friends Service Committee (AFSC) in Mānoa in the mid-1980s. Aloha to Ho'oipo DeCambra and Roy Takumi for all you taught me. More recently, Kyle Kajihiro at AFSC has been a comrade.

The Feminist Studies Department at the University of California, Santa Barbara supported me with a dissertation fellowship from 2004 to 2005, allowing me time to also complete the proposal for this book. Thanks especially to Eileen Boris, Leila Rupp, Laury Oaks, and Grace Chang for their mentorship.

My dissertation committee at the University of Hawai'i (UH) has been incredibly supportive of my research on haole, even post-dissertation. This book would not have been possible without David Stannard recommending me to the editors. Kathy Ferguson has provided unflagging support and guidance. Jon Goldberg-Hiller has encouraged me and championed the work. Noenoe Silva was extremely supportive and helpful with the research. Phyllis Turnbull read drafts of the manuscript and gave invaluable feedback. She has also been an incredible advocate for the project since day one.

Others at UH contributed to this work. Louise Kubo taught me to see the nuances of local identity, culture, and politics. RaeDeen Keahi-olalo Karasuda helped me to understand more about contemporary Kanaka Maoli issues and culture. Those in Noenoe Silva's Indigenous Politics class from spring 2003 deepened my knowledge of colonization and historical resistance. Masako Ikeda, Keith Leber, and Susan Corrado shepherded the manuscript through the process at UH Press. Paul Spickard has been amazing throughout, reading early drafts and being a font of support. Our meetings at a coffee shop in Goleta and frequent e-mails have always spurred me forward.

My San Francisco Bay Area comrades were always there to push me on and celebrate small milestones. So, too, with many of my colleagues in Ireland and the United States. My family has always supported the work, even before it was a book project. My father Marv Rohrer, brother Joby Rohrer, sister-in-law Kapua Kawelo, and niece and nephew Ho'o-hila Estella Kawelo and Kānehoalani Rohrer Kawelo have provided both support and inspiration. My mother Georgia K. Acevedo has served as my number-one research assistant, diligently clipping articles from local papers and keeping me up on island news. My partner, Dorrie Mazzone, has provided incredible emotional and intellectual support and assistance. The book would not have been completed if not for her confidence and love.

Mahalo nui loa to all of you!

# INTRODUCTION

*It's 1974. I'm seven. My hippie father has just moved our family from California to Kaua'i, one of the most rural of the Hawaiian Islands. I'm standing in the long lunch line outside the cafeteria at Kōloa Elementary school. I'm petrified—the school is huge, there are all sorts of rules, and the kids speak some form of English I can't understand. I've retreated into my head, allowing a gap to form in the line in front of me. The boy behind me gives me a push and says with complete disdain, "Fucking haole!" I have no idea what this means, but I know it can't be good.*

My introduction to haole came as a rude awakening, as it does for many. Growing up in California, I had some ideas about race. There were African American, Jewish, and Chicana/o children in the "free school" that my parents ran, and I ruled. If asked about race, I probably would have identified these children and their families and vocalized an antiracist sentiment learned from my parents, that is, "We should treat everyone the same regardless of skin color." It is unlikely that I would have racialized myself since, in my mind, race was not about me.

This all changed in that lunch line at Kōloa. I was suddenly a very distinct racial minority without any comprehension of what it meant. The kids around me pointed it out in some very direct, but also indirect, ways (there were whispers, glances, social exclusion). I was used to being liked, used to having many friends, so I was devastated and desperate to find some way to understand it all. I remember going home to talk to my mother about it. She said I should tell classmates I was Swedish, Swiss-German, Mexican, and Greek.

Emboldened with a renewed sense of self I made this declaration the

1

very next day on the playground, only to get the response, "So? You still one haole!" Clearly that was not going to work. I learned that "haole" was originally a native Hawaiian word meaning "foreign" that has come to mean white people and "acting white" or acting haole in the islands. Eventually I figured out how to diminish my haole quotient by trying not to call attention to myself and learning the ways of local culture. But the problem of being or becoming haole has never gone away. It has been one I have consciously returned to and often been forced to confront since Kōloa Elementary.

I begin with this story because I think the moment at which white people who move to Hawaiʻi are first racially marked as haole is pivotal. Confronted with the unfamiliar label "haole," we respond from what we know, and that is usually our experience of race on the continent (I refer to the continental United States as "the continent").[1] And so we are surprised because in Hawaiʻi we are made aware of our whiteness, whereas on the continent, for the most part, we were oblivious to it or took it for granted. Unlike the continent, whiteness in Hawaiʻi is always marked and often challenged. I do not mean to suggest that race on the continent is all one thing or that the "white experience" there is homogenous. There are, however, some common threads.

The most glaring thing about being white on the continent is its *non*experience. White Americans, for the most part, think we do not experience race; we think it is something that happens to other people, something that is not "our issue." We think race is primarily about Black people because that is what has been ingrained in us by our culture. We see ourselves as the nonraced norm because that is the message we constantly receive from the media, government, schools, corporations, and so forth. We do not see how we benefit from white privilege every day; we do not recognize our "possessive investment in whiteness" (Lipsitz 2006). As one scholar put it, "Racial privilege is the (non)experience of not being slapped in the face" (Frankenberg 1996, 4). This is changing somewhat in recent years as white people become more white-race cognizant, unfortunately often as they adopt ideas of white victimization espoused by anti-immigrant and anti-affirmative action rhetorics (Gallagher 1997). Still, overall, it is fair to say that white people on the continent tend not to think, or be challenged, about their whiteness.

As continental white people, we also have internalized the idea that it is not nice to talk about race, at least not publicly, and especially not in racially mixed company. It is commonly believed that talking about race or noticing race is a sign of racism—and above almost all else, we want to avoid being called racist. That does not mean we do not talk about race (especially when in the company of other white people), but we know that the polite thing to do is to be "colorblind," to ignore race (regardless of what we actually think about it). By not talking about it, we are also able to continue to pretend race—and therefore racism—do not exist.

And then we get to Hawai'i, where we are suddenly in the racial minority, which is uncomfortable or at least unusual for most of us, and all around us people are using racial terms and talking about race. Additionally, these people are not Black, the racialized "other" we are most familiar with, or rather think we are. They are Asian and Pacific Islanders, cultures we have come to think of as exotic, mysterious, or sinister. Hawai'i is one of only four "states" without a white majority, although haoles now make up over 40 percent of the population (California, New Mexico, and, most recently, Texas are the other three).[2] Native Hawaiians (Kanaka Maoli) make up approximately 20 percent of the population. In this book I use several terms for the indigenous people of Hawai'i: Kanaka Maoli, native Hawaiian, and Hawaiian. Kanaka Maoli is preferred politically because it comes from the Hawaiian language and carries ties to other indigenous Pacific people—"'Maoli' is cognate with 'Māori' of Aotearoa and 'Mā'ohi' of Tahiti" (Silva 2004, 13).[3] Kanaka Maoli trace their genealogies back to the time before Captain James Cook arrived in 1778. The balance of Hawai'i residents constitute the "local" (about 36.5 percent), excluding the 3.5 percent of the population who are military personnel (and hard to ignore are the seven to eight million tourists who visit each year but are not part of the census numbers).[4] When I talk about "locals" I do not mean residents. In Hawai'i, local identity and culture emerged primarily from the experience of laborers on sugar and pineapple plantations and is primarily a mix of Portuguese, Asian, native Hawaiian, and other Pacific Island cultures. There are many intralocal politics and differences that are important to think about and trace; however, this book deals mostly with the three overarching constructs of haole, native Hawaiian, and local. For newly arrived haoles, it is easy to feel like "strangers in a strange land," since in many ways that is what we are.

And yet a narrow focus on numbers reduces the complexity of haole, naturalizing it and obscuring the ways haole is a socially produced racial construction rooted in the colonization of Hawai'i. Sometimes "haole" is used as a descriptive marker, a way to identify us, especially for a local person who does not know us. For example, "Eh haole, you saw one set of keys ova hea?" Often, however, especially when we are new to the islands, we are called "haole" because we have acted out our haoleness, violating local cultural norms. This happens by being arrogant, rude, oblivious, greedy, talking too loud or too much, or taking up too much space. For example, consider this remark: "Eh haole, you can get off da phone an' move your cart from da middle of da aisle? Get odda folks like shop, you know!"

In the second example, it is obvious the speaker is upset. We quickly presume that their use of the word "haole" is meant negatively. But the first instance is more difficult to decipher because the speaker did not seem angry. Still, given the general white (non)experience with race, many haoles in this instance assume they have been slandered with a "dirty name." And then we start complaining about being called "haole," just like I did to my classmates at Kōloa Elementary. I further explore this question of whether or not "haole" is a derogatory word in chapter 3.

What I am trying to establish here is that when many white Americans come to Hawai'i, they interpret the meaning of haole through a continental lens: white is not raced but the norm; race is Black; and talking about race is impolite at best, racist at worst. This tendency to overlay a continental race relations framework on the islands is possible because, for the most part, Hawai'i is considered unproblematically part of the United States. Americans know very little about Hawai'i's history outside of the bombing of Pearl Harbor (although maybe this will change a little with native son Barack Obama in the White House). Instead, Hawai'i conjures up iconic images of white sand beaches, "hula girls," and umbrella drinks—images meant to seduce visitors into an ahistorical, apolitical bubble of a tropical paradise where they are eternally welcomed and comfortable.[5]

This book, then, is my latest effort to make some sense of haole and enter a more public discussion about the politics of haole. In the islands, people are used to identifying someone they do not know as "haole," but at the same time we also know it is much more complicated than that. Being haole is more than just having pale skin. We may have a niece who looks haole but acts completely local and has mixed ancestry. We know a local guy at work who is always being teased for acting haole. We have a local haole friend who grew up in Kekaha, Kauai, and speaks pidgin better than many urban locals. Haole reminds us that race is not phenotype or even genes (although it is often constructed that way). It can be as much about culture and behavior or performance as about skin color.

These examples demonstrate that race is a sociopolitical system used to classify people. Since race is a classification system we made up, and not something "natural" or given, it has history. In Hawai'i, it was forged in the fires of American colonialism that dispossessed Kanaka Maoli (native Hawaiians, those who were inhabiting the islands when Captain Cook arrived in 1778) and pitted different immigrant groups working on the plantations against one another. Given this history, it should not be surprising that race operates differently in the islands than it does on the continent, or anywhere else, for that matter. Race is very closely tied to place.

As with many racial-ethnic categories, it is impossible to neatly pin down what haole is. That is because it is many things all at once and these things change depending on time, space, and social context. By this I mean, for example, that haole is not the same thing now that it was during the time of the Hawaiian Kingdom; haole is not the same as honky or gringo, although they are related; and haole at Kamehameha Schools (established to benefit native Hawaiians) means something different than haole at Punahou School (established by missionary families and still predominantly haole). Haole is not something that just is, it is something that is an ongoing production; it is made and continually remade. It is best thought of as a verb rather than a noun. Therefore, I believe it is useful to think about how haole is produced, to look at the processes that operate that give haole meaning and power, and how they change. I have tried to structure this book to do that.

I draw from a variety of different sources in my investigation of haole: public controversy and debate (especially as chronicled in local media); cross-disciplinary academic scholarship; legal cases and discourse; and my own experience. By investigating these sources I hope to give a broad overview of the historic and contemporary constructions of haole. Part of the reason I cast such a wide net is that, to date, there has been very little scholarship about haole.

The sole existing book on the subject until now was written by Elvi Whittaker, a Canadian anthropologist, titled *The Mainland Haole: The White Experience in Hawaii* (1986). Whittaker visited Hawai'i in the early 1980s and interviewed over one hundred people, producing an insightful analysis of haole. Not having grown up in Hawai'i or having the experience of long-time residency, however, she misses some of the specificity of racial and indigenous politics in the islands. Her book was also written prior to much of the current Hawai'i scholarship I am able to draw upon. Inspired by Whittaker and other white feminists questioning their own whiteness, in 1997 I published an article on haole, drawing largely on my own personal experience (Rohrer 1997). There have been a few other pieces since then, but not many (Glenn 2002, Kraemer 2000, Ohnuma 2002, Pierce 2004).

This dearth of scholarship is contrasted with a good deal of "on the ground" discussion about, and knowledge of, haole. As already established, race is not the taboo subject in Hawai'i that it is in the dominant white culture of the continent. In fact, race gets talked about constantly in Hawai'i. It is now an everyday part of island culture, a tool people use to navigate a very multiracial environment. Yet, racial categorization is not indigenous to Hawai'i, but stems from a history of colonialism that dispossessed native Hawaiians, brought in a variety of mainly Asian and Pacific Islanders for plantation labor, and used race as a way to maintain power.

When I was writing my article in 1997 I was puzzled by how much scholarship there is about other racialized groups in the islands, but not haole. I now understand this as largely related to colonialism. Part of the way colonial power operates is by turning those who are not part of the colonizing group into "others"—those who are seen as different and inferior. In Hawai'i, this meant that haole (singular) became the standard, the norm against which others were measured. Academics, who are still mostly white even in Hawai'i, tend not to study themselves, but rather that which they deem to be abnormal, different, or a problem. By doing so, they can participate in that othering process. Māori scholar Linda Tuhiwai Smith instructs, "Problematizing the indigenous is a Western obsession" (Smith 1999, 91).

It follows that, until relatively recently, scholarship on Hawai'i has been dominated by non-Hawaiians (mostly haoles) studying "exotic" Hawai'i and its inhabitants. Native Hawaiians were characterized as savage, noble, lazy, unintelligent, generous, and exotic. Following a similar trajectory to representations of Native Americans, Kanaka Maoli were (and still are) represented as a tragic "dying breed"—a fascinating object for study by haoles, who for the most part were blind to their responsibility for Hawaiian dispossession and death. Additionally,

Asian immigrants were orientalized as a "yellow peril," un-American, and inassimilable. Unfortunately, there is still a lot of scholarship that explicitly or implicitly promotes these ideas.

Part of the goal of this book is to change that frame. Instead of continuing to cast an academic analytic gaze on "the other," I want to participate in moving the lens of interrogation to the haole. I study how haole colonization dispossessed Kanaka Maoli of power, land, and identity and how they resisted. I explore the complex relationships between haole, native Hawaiian, and local racial constructions. I look at the ongoing debate about the use of the term "haole" and the recent legal maneuvering to position haole as a victim.

Those who are familiar with postcolonial studies and critical whiteness studies will see the influences of these fields in this book. Postcolonial studies provides insight into thinking about the complex intersecting processes that constitute colonization, the relationships between people in colonies, and the many forms of resistance.[6] It has tended to focus on European imperialism, leaving U.S. imperialism undertheorized. Critical whiteness studies encourages us to think about whiteness as a form of racialization produced largely through the racialization of "others." It insists that without a better understanding of whiteness we cannot move toward racial justice.[7] As a field it has tended to focus on Black-white relations, given little attention to colonization, and encouraged an abstracted, essentialized notion of whiteness. I utilize the theoretical tools offered by both areas of scholarship, while at the same time trying to address some of their weaknesses.

This book is certainly not meant to be the definitive word on haole (there is something truly ironic about being identified as the "haole expert"). Rather, I hope it will add to conversations in the islands about how we think about haole, colonization, race relations, and struggles for Hawaiian sovereignty. At the end of the day I will be happy if I am able to raise questions regarding common assumptions about haole's place in Hawai'i and, further, Hawai'i's place in the United States.

## Roadmap

In chapter 1, "'Haole Go Home': Isn't Hawai'i Part of the U.S.?", I contextualize haole historically and politically as a colonial, and now neocolonial, form of American whiteness. I argue that it is impossible to understand haole without understanding something about Hawai'i's history of colonization. It is not my intent to give a full accounting of the colonization of Hawai'i (I point to some of the excellent literature in this area), but rather to give an overview of the colonial processes that brought haoles into nearly complete power during the century after the arrival of Captain Cook. These include the imposition of Western science, religion, law and politics, capitalism, and language and communication.

By mining some new Hawai'i scholarship, this chapter seeks to uproot some of the most pernicious misrepresentations of the colonization of the islands. It contests the ideas that Hawai'i's history began with Cook's landing, that colonization was easy and nonviolent, and, perhaps most importantly, that Kanaka Maoli did not resist. In this way it challenges notions of the haole as discoverer, savior, and civilizing force in the islands.

In chapter 2, "'No Ack!': What Is Haole, Anyway?", I explore the way haole is produced in relation to other racialized groups in Hawai'i; specifically, I look at the triangulation of haole, native Hawaiian, and local identities. I demonstrate how colonial racialization of native Hawaiians and nonwhite immigrants (locals) served to provide negative referents for haole. I discuss how many haoles today seek to be "anything but haole" (through denial, appropriation, and application of a color-blind ideology), but how local culture and politics simultaneously work to reinforce Hawaiian and local constructions of haole.

Further, I address how Hawaiian and local constructions of haole are based not just on an understanding of colonial history, but also on a particular set of attitudes and behaviors distinctly out of synch with native Hawaiian and local values and social norms. These include arrogance, ignorance about Hawai'i's history and cultures, greed (e.g., amassing wealth and taking up physical and social space), and the assumption of a stance of victimization in response to racial marking. While these attitudes and actions are often seen in haole newcomers, they are not limited to them.

Chapter 3, "'Eh, Haole': Is 'Haole' a Derogatory Word?", suggests that debating whether "haole" is a "dirty word"—a regular occurrence in the local media—is not particularly helpful. Instead, this chapter reframes the question to "What motivates people toward the continued use of 'haole' and what meanings does it mobilize?" Despite repetitive attempts to banish it, "haole" is still a popular word in local parlance precisely because people find it useful. It has not been replaced by the social-scientific term "Caucasian" as some would like because it carries particular meanings and histories rooted in Hawai'i.

Chapter 3 discusses two dominant discourses of race in Hawai'i, the well-known racial harmony, or "melting pot," narrative and a discourse of racial conflict and discrimination against nonlocals. While in some ways contradictory, in other ways these discourses reinforce one another in that they both naturalize haole's presence in Hawai'i. In the first, haole belongs to the racial stew of the islands as much as any other racialized group—it is "one of the tribe," to quote a haole playwright (Mark Pinkosh quoted in Viotti 1995). In the second, haole should be treated as any other group in Hawai'i but is unjustly discriminated against. Both discourses dehistoricize haole in that they pretend that over two hundred years of colonization do not exist, enabling haoles to position themselves as victims.

Chapter 4, "'Locals Only' and 'Got Koko?': Is Haole Victimized?", looks more closely at attempts in the last decade to recast haole as a victim. I argue that it is a mistake to equate entitlements, programs, or preferences for native Hawaiians with haole victimization. From the haole oligarchy that overthrew the Kingdom of Hawai'i and ruled the islands until the 1950s (when the "democratic revolution" put many Japanese locals into power),[8] to current statistics on the in-migration of haoles versus the out-migration of Hawaiians, to socioeconomic indicators, the pattern is one of variable but persistent haole political and economic power.

The spate of recent lawsuits, starting with the 2000 U.S. Supreme Court decision in *Rice v. Cayetano*, provides insight into how this power is now being reconsolidated through the overlay of dehistoricized colorblind ideology that whitewashes (pun intended) Hawai'i's history and makes Hawaiian claims for entitlements appear unreasonable. I demonstrate how these lawsuits misrepresent native Hawaiians as a racial group seeking "special rights" or "race-based" advantages rather than an indigenous people recognized in federal and state law. My hope is that by looking at haole through all these various lenses—historical, relational, performative, discursive, and material—a greater understanding of haole will emerge. This understanding will not reduce haole to simply the colonizer or a contemporary victim, but will look at the complex historical constructions, contestations, and discourses that have given haole meaning and power. Having a better understanding of haole is important for all who live in and/or care about these islands. We

cannot effectively address the ongoing processes of colonization, including militarism, tourism, and legal attacks on native Hawaiians, without
it. For those of us who recognize ourselves as haole, it is important that
we have this knowledge so we can begin to imagine how we might
become haole in different, and hopefully better, ways. We have to know
where we have been to know where we are going.

## A Note about Language

Throughout the book I use Hawaiian terms. They are not italicized as
they are not foreign to Hawai'i. They are defined at first use and I provide a glossary at the back. The spellings and definitions I use are based
on Mary Kawena Pukui and Samuel H. Elbert's *Hawaiian Dictionary*
(Pukui and Elbert 1986).

## CHAPTER I

# "HAOLE GO HOME"
## *Isn't Hawai'i Part of the U.S.?*

"Haole go home" was a popular slogan in the 1970s for a number of reasons. The native Hawaiian cultural and political revival was emerging and gaining strength, there was a strong antidevelopment movement in the islands, and local culture was finding new artistic expression, especially in literature, comedy, and music. It is not articulated as much these days, but the sentiment remains, clearly marking haole as not at home in Hawai'i. In contrast, white American visitors and newcomers to the islands are often surprised when they are called "haole" and when they encounter this sentiment. From their point of view, Hawai'i is the fiftieth state and they have just as much right to be here as any other U.S. citizen. They believe they can even move to Hawai'i and call it "home" if they want. The United States is, after all, "a free country."

It is this misunderstanding of Hawai'i and haole's relation to it that I want to challenge. This chapter asserts that there is no way to understand haole without understanding the colonization of Hawai'i. It is like trying to understand fish without studying the ocean. Haole makes no sense outside of Hawai'i, and contemporary Hawai'i makes no sense outside its colonial and, we could argue, now neocolonial history. And yet understanding Hawai'i's history is not a simple task precisely because the last two centuries of that history have been dominated by colonialism, which relies on its ability to "spin" its own story.

Until the early 1990s official Hawai'i history was based on scholarship done by haole historians who strung together a linear narrative of Western progress starting with Captain Cook's 1778 "discovery" and marching through the "civilizing" campaign of the missionaries, the "success" of plantation agriculture, the "unfortunate" demise of native people and power, and the "inevitable" Americanization of the government, which continued until the government *was* American with the culminating act of statehood in 1959. Native Hawaiian scholar Haunani-Kay Trask describes her epiphany about the dominant Hawai'i historiography taught her in school:

> Suddenly the entire sweep of our written history was clear to me. I was reading the West's view of itself through the degradation of my own past.
>
> . . . And when they said that our chiefs were despotic, they were telling of their own society, where hierarchy always results in domination. . . . And when they wrote Hawaiians were lazy, they meant that work must be continuous and ever a burden. . . . And when they wrote that we were superstitious, believing in the mana of nature and people, they meant that the West had long since lost a deep spiritual and cultural relationship to the earth.
>
> . . . For so long, more than half my life, I had misunderstood this written record, thinking it described my own people. (Trask 1993, 153–154)

New Hawai'i scholarship, especially that conducted by Kanaka Maoli scholars, is rewriting this dominant history by researching previously unknown or ignored historical documents, particularly those written in the Hawaiian language.[1] The importance of this scholarship cannot be overemphasized as it has caused a sea change in what story gets told about the last two centuries in Hawai'i. This chapter draws significantly on that new research and attempts to counter some of the most pernicious misrepresentations established and perpetuated by the dominant history.

My goal is to give a brief overview of the processes of colonization that wrested power from native Hawaiians and transferred it to haoles. These processes worked through the Western institutions of science, religion, law and politics, capitalism, and language and communication. Those who are familiar with other colonial struggles will see commonalities with other colonial histories. More scholarship needs to be done drawing Hawai'i into broader discussions of colonialism and neocolonialism. Significantly, I am looking at specific processes of colonization in the islands, focusing on the hundred-plus years between Cook's arrival and annexation.

Often colonization is conceived of as one thing (takeover of territory for resource extraction and empire building), accomplished through one mode (the use of force), and occurring uni-directionally (from colonizer onto colonized). Actually, colonization is many things (occupation of territory, yes, but also political, economic, religious, and cultural usurpation), accomplished as much by strategic accumulation of power as by direct force, and occurring relationally with complex, unpredictable actions and responses from all involved. This means that colonization is never totalizing. As native Hawaiian scholar Noenoe Silva writes, "As power persists so does resistance, finding its way like water slowly carving crevices into and through rock" (Silva 2004, 163). As strong as the hegemony was that haoles built in the century after Cook, it was never complete—there were always cracks, always resistances, and there continue to be.

## Western Science: Redefining Hawai'i

One of the key ways colonization works is by overlaying the colonizer's framework or systems of meaning on the colonized place. U.S. citizens take for granted our understanding of Hawai'i as a volcanic chain of islands in the middle of the Pacific Ocean discovered by Captain Cook in 1778 and logically annexed to the United States, yet this understanding was constructed as part of colonization. It is no more "real" or "true" than other understandings of Hawai'i among native Hawaiians, other Pacific Islanders, or Asian immigrants. It is just that the colonizing haole had the power to declare its truth.

Let us take some time thinking about this definition of Hawai'i, starting with the assertion that the islands were "discovered" by Captain Cook. The moment of discovery is the point at which history starts for a place; indeed, most histories of Hawai'i start at Cook's landing. We know that to discover something, you must be the first person to find it. What, then, are we supposed to think about the thriving population of native people already in the islands when Cook arrived? We know they were there because Cook wrote about them at great length. The trick was they did not count in the eyes of the West as fully human, and certainly not as "discoverers" themselves.

To count as a discoverer on the high seas at the time, you had to have the technologies of Western science that enable discovery: maps, compasses, spyglasses, written reports and communication from other captains, and, of course, large sailing ships. Native Hawaiians had none of these tools; they used other means for their navigation. Not only did they not count as discoverers, but they were also not seen as fully human because they lacked the trappings of Western civilization—clothing, one god, capitalism, patriarchy, technology, written language, and so forth. As a result, they were simply categorized as part of the "natural" scenery, "primitives" in a savage state.

And so, Western science helped make it possible for Captain Cook to claim to have discovered Hawai'i and that became the story that continues to be told today. The impact of that story is tremendous, especially for Kanaka Maoli, because it vanishes centuries of their habitation and their understanding of how they came to be in the islands. Kanaka Maoli tell a different story about Cook. They describe 1778 as the time when the islands discovered Captain Cook lost in the Pacific Ocean. Note that Kanaka Maoli do not say *they* found Cook, but that the islands "discovered" him, thus asserting the agency and life of the land (Michael Kahikina as quoted in Milner and Goldberg-Hiller 2002, 33). The 'āina, the land, in their view is alive—it can do things, want things, and know things. They, in fact, are the offspring of a union between the earth and sky, making the 'āina a direct relative. Where we who are non-Hawaiian see a volcanic chain of islands and/or the "50th state," Kanaka Maoli see familial relation. Beginning to comprehend these fundamental differences in ways of seeing and knowing is at the heart of understanding haole.

Kanaka Maoli wove, and continue to recover and weave, an intricate and dynamic web of ontology, cosmology, epistemology, and genealogy that includes interplay between gods, land, ocean, wind, sky, people, ancestors, plants, and animals. Much has been lost, destroyed, or translated out of contemporary understandings of this weave, but we know enough to know that colonization caused, and continues to cause, a violent and radical tear in that weave, a disruption, a "dismemberment."[2] Kanaka Maoli saw no bright line between people and place, between past and present. If the land was the people and the people the land, if elaborate genealogies traced ancestors flowing back across and through time and space, then the imposition of Western geography and cartography—which is all about boundaries—caused literal dismemberment:

> Hawaiian identity is, in fact, derived from the Kumulipo, the great cosmogonic genealogy. Its essential lesson is that every aspect of the Hawaiian conception of the world is related by

birth, and as such, all parts of the Hawaiian world are one indivisible lineage. Conceived in this way, the genealogy of the Land, the Gods, Chiefs, and people intertwine with one another, and with all myriad aspects of the universe. (Kameʻeleihiwa 1992, 2)

This is clearly very different from the way Western science understands the land, which leads to another colonizing process employed through science: the transformation of the ʻāina into land. Rather than something alive and dynamic, haoles imposed their science on the place we know of as Hawaiʻi to turn it into something static to be claimed, owned, and exploited. One of the misrepresentations of this history is that Hawaiʻi peacefully transformed into a modern place. Yet this erases the cultural and physical violence done to the people and the land and the continuing resistance to that violence.

Geography and cartography were called upon to impose "order" on the islands, to fit them into the Western frame, to map them, thus putting them within the Western imperial grasp. And so it was that, within a few decades of "discovery," the major Western powers were vying for control over them. In fact, anticipating this, Captain Cook was instructed by the English Crown to make sure to distribute "Things as will remain as Traces and Testimonies of your having been there" (as quoted in Herman 1995, 63). In other words, "make sure to pee in the corners so that other imperialists will know we got there first."

The mapping of Hawaiʻi also did violence by renaming and transforming specific places. A Western grid was imposed on a place previously organized organically and not controlled by straight lines but by relationship to place (islanders today resist this imposition by giving directions using specific places and events as markers rather than the four cardinal directions). Getting from point A to point B was the colonizers' the goal, not attending to things along the way or participating in natural cycles. Roads and buildings were built and Hawaiian place names were lost or replaced with westernized names, severing deep relationships with genealogies, uses, and moʻolelo (story, tale, legend). For Hawaiians, every place had a name and a significance, and specific stories connected it to other places and to themselves. Without the names to recall these relationships, they are quickly lost, paved over in the name of progress.

Burgeoning agricultural science was used to justify the turning of "wasted land" into huge sugar and pineapple plantations owned by haole businessmen (often former missionaries who turned from saving souls to saving soil from "underutilization"). Hawaiian tending of the 'āina balanced ecological diversity, sustenance crop cultivation, gathering techniques, use of natural topography, and labor efficiency with a deep respect and honoring of place. Plantation agriculture called for the huge production of monocrops at almost any ecological, social, or spiritual price.

Industrial agriculture also ushered in a new discourse about "lazy" Hawaiians. Prior to this, haoles had reported on the sophisticated methods of cultivation and land management used by the Hawaiians. They marveled at the efficiency of a system where everyone had enough food, where food was well distributed to keep diets balanced (fish, kalo, limu, fruit, etc.), and where no one had to labor more than four hours a day to keep it all running smoothly. The story changed when it became clear how much money there was to be made off of sugar and pineapple. Increasingly, haoles wrote about the travesty of "wasted" or "underutilized land" and about Hawaiians who wanted only to lie around, play music, hula, or surf rather than cultivate surplus crops. This discourse helped pave the way for the radical change from ali'i (chief, chiefess)-controlled, communally tended 'āina to the establishment of private property.

## Religion

Religion played a key role in the colonization of Hawai'i, particularly during 1820–1850, when missionary activities were at their height. Key to understanding the strength of the missionary agenda are the interrelated elements of traditional Kanaka Maoli sociopolitical structure; the horror of mass deaths during this period; the role religion played in fortifying Western social, political, and economic ideologies and structures; and the foundation religion laid for subsequent control of the islands by a missionary-planter oligarchy.

As discussed, Kanaka Maoli operated with an integrated worldview that wove together creation, genealogy, power, nature, divinity, and leadership. Because they saw themselves as related to the land, each other, and the gods, Kanaka Maoli drew no distinct boundaries between social, political, and spiritual spheres; each was part and parcel of the other (there was clearly a system of social ranking, but that system itself crossed these planes). Thus, as the Hawaiian sociopolitical structure began to unravel as a consequence of foreign intervention in the first decades after Cook, so too did Hawaiian spiritual beliefs. This crisis of faith was the catalyst for breaking the sacred gender-segregated eating kapu (taboo, prohibition) (Osorio 2002, 11). This dramatic break with the long-standing "religion" in turn spiraled the people into further crisis.

At the heart of the crisis was the horrific depopulation of native Hawaiians described as "the Great Dying" and primarily attributable to multiple diseases brought by foreigners to which Kanaka Maoli had no immunity (the Hawaiian islands are the most "isolated" land masses on the planet, making their biodiversity unique and fragile). Scholars estimate that by the end of the nineteenth century the thriving population that inhabited the islands at Cook's landing had decreased by 95 percent (Osorio 2002, 9–10; Stannard 1989). This powerfully demonstrates how colonialism can be seen as a form of genocide in Hawai'i.

The American missionaries, who arrived in 1820, five months after the ending of the eating kapu, exploited this crisis by offering The Answer—conversion and adoption of strict Calvinist discipline. "The church became an institution offering life when death was everywhere, and the eventual conversion of Hawaiians by the thousands must be understood in the context of a time when their own religion, akua, and Ali'i could not prevent them from dying" (Osorio 2002, 12).

Conversion meant an extreme reordering of Kanaka Maoli lifestyle and ideology. Following the broad missionary agenda, it meant becoming "civilized" by becoming Westernized. It meant adopting Western clothing, family structure, domesticity, sexual mores, work ethics, social etiquette, educational systems, parenting practices, and so forth. Missionary documents, especially those written by missionary women, who were the primary force in this civilizing project, are full of descriptions of their efforts on these accounts, and quite often their frustrations (Grimshaw 1989, xxii). It was this adoption of Western culture, not simply religious beliefs, that was supposed to "save" the Kanaka Maoli and make them "successful."

Resistance to missionary consolidation of power took a variety of forms, from mimicry and evasion, to playing foreign powers off one another, to violence. Many Kanaka Maoli, especially the maka'āinana (commoner, general populace), were ambivalent about conversion and became increasingly upset about expanding missionary power. By the 1840s missionaries were discouraged that they were not making the "deep" change they had hoped for. They complained that the Hawaiians were evasive and just paying lip service to Christian principles, concluding that they were hopelessly stuck in their heathen ways.

The missionaries could not see their own contradictions, although they were increasingly apparent to the Kanaka Maoli. The discourse of the "noble savage" (transplanted from encounters with native peoples on the continent) collided with notions of the Kanaka Maoli as "heathens," creating a tension in which native Hawaiians were simultaneously worthy of saving and inherently damned. Reverend Hiram Bingham, one of the most influential Calvinist missionaries, published a memoir in 1849 after returning to New England. As one who never had much faith in the "natives" to begin with, he wrote, "By what means shall the knowledge of the arts and sciences be acquired by a nation so stupid and ignorant, whose destination seemed almost to forbid their progress, while it imperatively required it, and whose spiritual wants, first to be met, demanded more attention than the missionaries could give?" (Bingham 1969, 171).

Having been the first organized grouping of haoles on the ground, the missionary families were able to establish their dominance early on. The moral authority they marshaled as a consequence of their religious position, their contact with the culture, and friendships with the aliʻi opened up untold opportunities, especially in government and the acquisition of land. And so, when the money to be made in sugar and pineapple became apparent, many missionaries, and missionary sons, became planters.

> In Hawaiʻi, the missionaries turned these values [Calvinist Puritan] into immense profits through the plantation economy. Their ideology necessarily included a firm conviction of their own superiority, and thus they saw little contradiction in becoming the owners of the land and overseers of the production while the people they had come to save labored and lived in poverty. (Silva 2004, 52–53)

## Law and Politics

Legal and political processes were centrally important in colonization and the establishment of haole hegemony in the century after contact, and those processes continue to be paramount today. In this section I touch on the initial transformation to Western law; the Māhele; the period of the overthrow, provisional government, and Republic; and annexation. Within each of these moments, contradiction and resistance is present, reminding us of the instability of colonization.

Kanaka Maoli governed themselves successfully for centuries before Western contact in a complex system founded on the principles of balance (pono), spiritual-political power (mana), responsibility (kuleana), connectedness, and reciprocity between people, chiefs, gods, and natural forces. It was not a romanticized utopia; there were problems, violence, and repression, but the culture was founded in a deep reciprocity. King Kamehameha I consolidated rule of all of the islands in 1810 with the help of Western guns. There was no written law until a Declaration of Rights in 1839, and a constitution one year later transformed the Kingdom of Hawai'i into a constitutional monarchy. (Kanaka Maoli operated within an oral tradition until the missionaries developed a written Hawaiian language.)[3]

Haole historians have misclassified precontact Hawai'i as "feudal" and told a seamless story of "gradual and voluntary" change with the ali'i simply asking Americans for help in establishing a Western legal system (Trask 1993, 150–152). New research shows messier, contested processes stoked by power, desire, death, and disease. Factors leading to the acceptance of Western law and political structure include some already mentioned and others: the devastation of disease; the disintegration of the traditional social and political structure and the subsequent desire to reestablish pono; the introduction of Western military technology; the increasing debt of the ali'i; the influence of the missionaries; and the demands of foreign residents and their respective governments, including threats on the independence of the kingdom (Merry 2000, Osorio 2002).

As imperial powers took increasing interest in the islands, the ali'i were placed in a difficult position as they tried to maintain the respect of the gods and their people, while garnering it from outside nations. The ali'i made strategic decisions to model their kingdom and themselves after Western powers: they adopted Western law and increasingly relied on haole advisers; they built and furnished a palace similar to those in Europe; they educated themselves to the hilt; and they took on all the obligations and trappings of Victorian monarchs (racking up considerable debt) (Merry 2000, Osorio 2002). Still, between 1820 and 1843, the United States, Britain, and France all at some point threatened or took military action against the island nation (Wood 1999, 9). By the mid-1840s the Kingdom of Hawai'i had negotiated treaties recognizing its independence with all the major Western and Asian powers, but challenges by resident foreigners and threats of imperial takeover continued (Merry 2000, 87).

The maka'āinana protested these changes because they worried about the increasing power of the haole and the detrimental impact on their leaders and themselves. They saw clearly the paradox that ensnared their leaders.

> This is the sovereignty paradox of the late 1840s: in order to produce a government able to deal with the foreign residents and to gain respectability in the eyes of the imperialist foreign community, the leaders adopted the forms of modern government and rule of law, but these forms required foreigners skilled in their practices to run them. And as foreigners developed and ran these new bureaucratic systems of law and government, they redefined the Hawaiian people as incapable, naturalizing this incapacity in racialized terms. (Merry 2000, 89)

The most devastating sociolegal event for Hawaiians occurred with the Māhele, a series of laws enacted between 1845 and 1850 that transformed the communal land system into private property.[4] The first sugar plantation had opened in 1835, and the potential for profit was soon apparent but clearly could not be fulfilled without the ability to own land.[5] Haoles in power ramped up their rhetoric about the sin of "wasted land" and wove in a new thread insisting that the cure to Hawaiian "indolence" was to allow the "poor kanaka" to become king of his own manor. If Hawaiians could own their own small plots they would become invested in its maximum utilization (Herman 1995).

Just as the maka'āinana had predicted, the Māhele ended up benefiting the haole and dispossessing the native peoples. Within fifteen years of the new laws, nearly 75 percent of the land on O'ahu was owned by haoles (McGregor 1989, 82). (Rates of haole ownership on other islands are difficult to determine, but it is likely they were also high, although not as high as O'ahu, where the majority of haoles were located.) There were two primary factors for this discrepancy. First, the haole were quite familiar with laws dealing with private property and were quickly able to use them to their advantage, especially since they helped write them.

Second, the maka'āinana were suspicious of, and anxious about, this radical change in their sociopolitical structure. The ali'i and akua (god, goddess) had always managed the land and taken care of them. They were not eager to sever those relationships and replace them with a foreign concept of ownership that contradicted their worldview (Osorio 2002, 53–54).

By the time of the overthrow of the monarchy there was a wide-ranging discourse regarding Kanaka Maoli's inherent inability to govern themselves. This discourse was built on the mistaken notion of a feudal traditional society, "evidence" of Hawaiians' failure to adapt to capitalist culture, and a narrative—honed through the colonization of the continent—about the tragic but inevitable disappearance of native peoples in the wake of white "civilization." At worst, the discourse was flagrantly racist, and at best paternalistic; either way, it supported one conclusion: law and politics were the domain of the white man—it was time for Hawaiians to stop playing government. And so on January 16, 1893, a group of haole conspirators deposed Queen Lili'uokalani with the assistance of U.S. Minister John Stevens, who ordered the landing of U.S. Marines. The next day the coup leaders announced the end of the Hawaiian monarchy and declared themselves the "provisional government" of Hawai'i.

The queen stepped down under protest, strategically yielding to the U.S. government, not the coup leaders, and urging her people not to fight back with force. She wanted to avoid bloodshed and was convinced that when the U.S. government heard what had happened, they would put it right. Her protest read, in part, "I yield to the superior force of the United States of America . . . until such time as the Government of the United States shall, upon the facts being presented to it, undo the action of its representatives, and reinstate me in the authority which I claim as the constitutional sovereign of the Hawaiian Islands" (Liliuokalani 1964, 365).

President Harrison was not sympathetic to the queen's protest and immediately sent an annexation treaty to the Senate as desired by the haole conspirators. The treaty was withdrawn a month later by incoming President Cleveland, who determined that the queen's protest should be taken seriously. Cleveland appointed Congressman James H. Blount to the position of U.S. Special Commissioner in the Department of State and sent him to the islands to carry out a thorough investigation. Upon arrival, to the dismay of the coup leaders, Blount sent the U.S. troops back onto their ship, dismissed Minister Stevens back to the continent, and lowered the U.S. flag that had been raised over ʻIolani Palace. He then embarked on an extensive investigation, culminating in a report of over one thousand pages commonly known as the "Blount Report" (Coffman 1998, 142).

In December 1893, after reviewing the Blount Report, President Cleveland addressed Congress, calling the coup "an act of war" and therefore urging the restoration of Queen Liliʻuokalani to her throne. But the Congress was not so sure, Cleveland was voted out of office, and years of debate ensued in which the U.S. conversation was reframed as a question of annexation or not, neatly obscuring the illegal overthrow. Advocates on both sides used racist arguments, with the pro-annexationists continuing their rhetoric about how Hawaiians were "incapable" of civilized government and how Americans in Hawaiʻi needed protection. The anti-annexationists stirred up white racial fears about incorporating such an overwhelmingly nonwhite territory into the union.[6]

Upon realizing that annexation was not going to be immediate, the haoles in the provisional government scrambled to set up what they called a "republic" and wrote a new constitution. They set strict voting requirements based on property ownership, naturalization, and facility with English or Hawaiian in order to exclude an increasing population of Asian immigrants. On top of that, they required an oath of loyalty to the new illegal government—an oath that many Kanaka Maoli refused to take. "The monarchy had been overthrown to enhance the interest of a few, not to bring about democracy to the population at large. Hence the rebel government . . . moved quickly to disfranchise virtually all nonwhites and supporters of the former monarch" (Bell 1984, 29).

One of the most destructive ideas perpetuated by haole historians is that the Hawaiian people did little or nothing to resist the overthrow. This is what I learned in seventh grade when I took the required course on "Hawaiiana" at Kōloa Elementary School. It stood as official "truth" until Hawaiian language scholar and political scientist Noenoe Silva decided to investigate in the early 1990s. (There was always a counter-discourse kept alive in stories of kupuna [grandparent, ancestor] about resistance, but these stories were discounted for lack of "evidence" until Silva's research.) Silva did something that seems obvious but had not yet been done: she studied the wealth of documents in the Hawaiian language, especially newspapers, written at the time of the overthrow. What she found was that these sources were filled with resistance and news of resistance (Silva 2004). In fact, she argues that the writing in and of itself was a form of strong resistance.

While the U.S. Congress was engaged in its own bigoted, self-serving debate over whether or not to bring Hawai'i "under Uncle Sam's wing" and the haole oligarchy worked to seize even more power, Kanaka Maoli and others supportive of the constitutional government were organizing all forms of creative protest. They wrote to the newspapers, they held rallies, they organized their civic clubs, they refused to support churches or businesses involved or complicit in the coup, and they found ways to support Queen Lili'uokalani, even while she was held prisoner in her own palace (Silva 2004). One of the most impressive things they did was gather 38,000 signatures of Hawaiian nationals on petitions to the U.S. Congress protesting annexation. Even allowing for some duplication, this is over 90 percent of the total population of 40,000 (Silva 2004, 151). This shatters the idea that the Hawaiian people did not care about the overthrow or that they secretly welcomed it.

These petitions, known as the Kū'ē petitions, were delivered to Congress by a delegation from the islands before an 1897 vote on annexation. The petitions and the force of the delegates' arguments succeeded in changing many senators' minds, thereby defeating the treaty (Silva 2004, 156). A year later, however, Congress used the pretext of the war with Spain in the Philippines to annex the islands. Since the pro-annexationists knew they still did not have the two-thirds votes needed for an annexation treaty, annexation was illegally pushed through with a joint resolution known as the Newlands Resolution (Silva 2004, 160).

The resurfacing of the Kū'ē petitions—which had been in the U.S. National Archives all along and simply ignored by haole historians (Silva 2004, 163)—and the other evidence of resistance has had an incredible impact on Kanaka Maoli and on the historiography of Hawai'i. Silva and a new generation of Hawai'i scholars are turning the old history on its head, showing how much Hawaiian resistance existed and how effectively Kanaka Maoli used the democratic process, demonstrating their faith that justice would be achieved and belying the stereotype about their "backwardness" and inability to govern. This evidence reinvigorated the movement for Hawaiian sovereignty. Kanaka Maoli activist and scholar Lynette Cruz articulates the new sentiment: "As our ancestors, by their signatures on the great petitions, stood by their country and by their queen in time of trouble, so must we continue to claim what, by law, by history, by culture and spirit, is ours. We are a Living

Nation because the Hawaiian people . . . continue to live—as a nation, as a country" (Lynette Cruz as quoted in Silva 2004, 163).

## Capitalism

A discussion of haole colonization would not be complete without a discussion of capitalism, the backbone of the haole oligarchy. From the early fur,[7] sandalwood, and whale trade, to sugar and pineapple and then tourism, haoles pursued profit making with a vengeance. Early visitors noted that Kanaka Maoli had sophisticated agricultural and ocean harvesting systems and could feed themselves well with a few hours' work in the loʻi (fishponds) each day. "Supply and demand," "surplus," and "profit" were literally foreign concepts. Eloquently grasping the clash of cultures, Samuel Mānaiakalani Kamakau wrote at the time, "You foreigners regard the winds, the rain, the land, and the sea as things to make money with; but we look upon them as loving friends with whom we share the universe" (as quoted in Kent 1983, 14). Kamakau was an early graduate of one of the missionary schools and became a respected historian, teacher, and politician. His histories were published in newspapers and are one of the fullest sources of information on Hawaiian society before haole dominance (Silva 2004, 16–17; Osorio 2002, 3–5).[8]

With the influx of foreigners, however, the aliʻi became interested in acquiring Western goods: weapons, ironwork, clothing, technology, and all forms of manufactured items. Barter and trade worked for a bit, but soon the aliʻi wanted accumulated wealth. Historians enumerate multiple aliʻi desires: to hold on to their nation by proving it was as civilized as any other, to make their people proud, to increase their mana, and to possess beautiful objects and riches of the East and West. One of the early consequences of this complicated weave of desires was that the makaʻāinana were compelled by King Kamehameha I to leave their loʻi to work for months at a time to cut sandalwood, as it was highly prized in Asia. This disruption in traditional cultivation led to famine and accelerated the Kanaka Maoli mass dying and social upheaval (McGregor 1989, 78–79; Kent 1983, 20).

Sandalwood forests were virtually wiped out by 1820, and the whaling trade stepped up as the next moneymaking enterprise. With it came more foreign traders with more diseases and more merchants eager to sell. Lahaina and Honolulu became raucous port towns where prostitution flourished and accelerated the spread of disease. "Whaling had a much greater impact on Island economic and social structure than did sandalwood. For the first time, the Hawaiian masses were drawn into a cash economy as workers and producers on a regular basis" (Kent 1983, 22). Significant as these early trading enterprises were, it was the arrival of the missionaries and their subsequent interest in sugar that was bound to have the greatest long-term impact on the Hawaiian economy and political future.

The rise of the sugar industry in Hawaiʻi has been well chronicled and analyzed. It drove politics in Hawaiʻi for one hundred years from the 1840s onward, including the reciprocity treaty with the United States, the overthrow of the monarchy, and the campaigns for annexation and eventual statehood. The phrase "King Cane" became true in more ways than one.

> Hawaiian society came to be organized around sugar production. Ground and ocean transportation, utilities, housing, imports of food and retail items: all revolved around the development of the sugar industry. It was the sugar industry, whose lifeline was the U.S. market, that bound Hawaii to the U.S. and ultimately led to its incorporation into the United States. (McGregor 1989, 81)

By 1883, haoles controlled 92 percent of plantation interests in Hawaiʻi and were raking in enormous profits (McGregor 1989, 82). With the rise of sugar came the importation of massive numbers of laborers from Portugal, Puerto Rico, China, Japan, Korea, the Philippines, and, later, other locations in Asia and the Pacific Islands. With these waves of immigrants came a drastic shift in the population of the islands that was destined to become the backdrop of every facet of Hawaiʻi politics from then on.[9] As a means of maintaining power and control, the haole oligarchy set up strict racial divisions within the plantations, with separate jobs, pay scales, and segregated housing, or "camps," for each group. The planters also established a harsh penal contract system through the Masters' and Servants' Act (1850) and participated in all forms of coercive and inhumane labor practices. The overthrow of the Kingdom of Hawaiʻi formally put haoles in the driver's seat.

A visiting National Labor Relations Board representative remarked in 1937 that what the haoles liked to call plantation paternalism was just another form of "fascism" (Fuchs 1961, 49). "The immigrants were regarded by the plantation elite as less than fully human, as interchange-able cogs in the productive apparatus—as *commodities* to produce com-modities" (Kent 1983, 40; emphasis in original). Ronald Takaki graphi-cally illustrates this by uncovering original requisitions from plantation managers to their suppliers that include "lists of orders for men and materials" (Takaki 1983, 23). One such order lists "Filipinos" alphabeti-cally after "Fertilizer" (Takaki 1983, 24).

Resistance to these conditions was always present in the form of work slowdowns, songs, cane fires resulting from arson, desertion, and strikes. Unions were segregated racially and, at first, went on strike sep-arately. In 1920 plantation organizers moved beyond "blood unionism" and the Japanese and Filipino unions struck together. With 77 percent of the Oʻahu work force on strike, plantation operations ground to a halt. The experience led to the first interracial unions in Hawaiʻi that more effectively took on the capitalist haole power structure (Takaki 1983, 153–176).

## Language and Communication

I have already hinted at the importance of language and communication in haole colonization (e.g., naming the illegal government a "republic," calling precontact society in Hawaiʻi "feudal," etc.). Here I address two processes of colonization that mobilized language and communications: the dismissal of the oral tradition of Kanaka Maoli and the establish-ment of a written language, and the battle over which newspaper(s) would reign as the major communication vehicle in the islands.

In an unusually sensitive description of Kanaka Maoli oral tradi-tion, Eleanor Nordyke writes, "The unwritten literature of pre-contact Hawaiʻi was transferred from one generation to the next by carefully trained storytellers who received knowledge through their ears as soci-eties that use the written word receive information through their eyes" (Nordyke 1989, 13). In contrast, Reverend Hiram Bingham wrote in his memoir (first published in 1847): "In place of authentic history they had obscure oral traditions, national or party songs, rude narra-tives of successions of kings, wars, victories, exploits of gods, heroes, priests, sorcerers, the giants of iniquity and antiquity, embracing con-jecture, romance, and the general absurdities of Polytheism" (Bing-ham 1969, 2). The haole historical canon almost uniformly dismisses Kanaka Maoli precontact history as inconsequential, if it acknowl-edges it at all. Mele (song), moʻolelo (story), and oli (chant), most of which included elaborate genealogies, were not considered worthy historical record. Lilikalā Kameʻeleihiwa counters, "The genealogies are the Hawaiian concept of time, and they order space around us. Through them we learn of the exploits and identities of our ancestors" (Kameʻeleihiwa 1992, 19).

The missionaries made it one of their first tasks to capture ka ʻōlelo ʻōiwi (the Kanaka Maoli language) on paper, inevitably vanishing much of its nuance and fluidity. This was a mixed blessing for the Kanaka Maoli: it contributed to the demise of the oral tradition, it allowed for more rapid conversion to Christianity and subsequent abandonment of traditional culture, and yet it also allowed for more efficient communication and therefore resistance. (The 1896 provisional government ban of spoken Hawaiian from public schools can be seen as part of this effort to diminish Hawaiian oral tradition.) Having produced the written language, the missionaries put it right to work: "For forty years the mission controlled the power of the printed word in Hawaiʻi. The missionaries used this power not just to save souls but to assist in the progress of plantation/colonial capitalism, to control public education, to mold government into Western forms and to control it, and to domesticate Kanaka women" (Silva 2004, 54–55).

In addition to controlling everything printed in Hawaiian, the missionary elite owned and controlled the English-language newspapers. The press was dominated by Henry Whitney, and then Lorrin Thurston's *Pacific Commercial Advertiser*, which was established in 1856 and was the precursor to today's *Honolulu Advertiser*. This paper was a mouthpiece for the haole elite. It railed against the monarchy, degraded the Kanaka Maoli, promoted capitalism, congratulated the oligarchy, and obsessed over what to do about the "yellow peril."

According to Noenoe Silva, a "war of newspapers" emerged in Hawaiʻi once Kanaka Maoli began publishing their own newspaper in 1861. "To the shock and outrage of the missionary establishment, a group of Kānaka Maoli, makaʻāinana, and aliʻi together, transformed themselves into speaking subjects proud of their Kanaka ways of life and traditions and unafraid to rebel" (Silva 2004, 55). In a continuation of the oral tradition, the Kanaka Maoli papers published mele and moʻolelo. The haoles immediately proclaimed the first of these papers to therefore be publishing "obscenities" and tried to shut it down. When that failed, the haoles began publishing their own Hawaiian-language newspaper to compete and continued to try to censor the content of the Kanaka Maoli papers. And so it went—a perfect illustration of the struggles of power and resistance inherent in colonial processes.[10]

Newspapers became extremely important as a communication tool for the Hawaiians. By midcentury, literacy in Hawai'i was nearly universal, and the Kanaka Maoli press easily gained the largest circulation in the islands. Papers helped spread news more quickly between islands and allowed for uncensored expression of nationalist sentiment. Silva shows how this was underscored during Queen Lili'uokalani's imprisonment (Silva 2004, 187–191).

The queen was prohibited from having newspapers, so Kanaka Maoli would bring her flowers carefully wrapped in the latest paper. Those papers contained elaborate mele with kaona (hidden meaning, concealed reference) that contained messages to the queen (Silva 2004, 8). Frequently these were messages of support, encouraging the queen not to despair, that her people were with her. Only those fluent in the language and culture could interpret these many layers of meaning. Queen Lili'uokalani would write back using kaona, and her writings were smuggled out and printed for all to read (but only some to understand).[11]

## Contemporary Colonialism

While this chapter mostly deals with the period between 1778 and annexation in 1898, colonization is not a thing of the past in Hawai'i. Since the islands became officially (but not legally) part of the United States, the colonial processes of domination and exploitation have evolved into less overt, more neocolonial forms. While religion has lost the power it once had, it ushered in and made space for the other processes of colonialization. In fact, the consolidation of power by the haole oligarchy in the islands reached its apex during the first half of the twentieth century, putting a stranglehold on economics, politics, education, and social structure. Lawrence Fuchs instructs,

> No community of comparable size on the mainland was controlled so completely by so few individuals for so long. Rarely were political, economic, and social controls simultaneously enforced as in Hawaii. Rarely were controls so personal. . . . Hawaii's oligarchy skillfully and meticulously spun its web of control over the Islands' politics, labor, and economic institutions, without fundamental challenge. (Fuchs 1961, 152)

The center of oligarchic power was what has come to be known as the "Big Five" corporations: Castle and Cooke, C. Brewer, American Factors, Theo H. Davies, and Alexander and Baldwin. Fuchs gives a good deal of attention to the Big Five in *Hawaii Pono,* as does Noel Kent in *Hawaii: Islands under the Influence* (1983). Instead of competing with each other, the corporate managers consolidated power via a model of cooperation held together through interlocking directorates and overlapping social and familial circles. Significantly, by 1935 one-third of all directors and officers of sugar plantations and related businesses were direct missionary descendants (Fuchs 1961, 249). Not content with merely controlling the sugar industry, these haole businessmen expanded their empire into transportation (shipping and local rail), banking, insurance, utilities, and wholesale and retail enterprises. They held legislative power in the territory, maintained through the suppression and manipulation of the local vote. With this political power they used the government to maintain their dominance by structuring policies to their advantage and as a tool of repression. Noel Kent writes, "The government deliberately frustrated land reform in order to continue the policy of huge public land rental by the plantations at nominal rents. It diverted public water to irrigate sugar plantation fields free of charge; it used the police and national guard to break strikes and suppress working-class agitation" (Kent 1983, 77). The Big Five and broader haole oligarchy held control in the islands until well into the 1940s, when World War II, declining sugar profits, and air travel worked to begin the loosening of their singular hold.

Colonization post-annexation was also carried out via public education. Since nearly all haole children attended private schools, not much official attention was given to public schools during the early territorial period. However, remnants of missionary interest in education and haole paternalism remained, especially among haole wives, and whatever consideration was given to public schools came from them (Fuchs 1961, 265–267).

Public education received heightened scrutiny after World War I and into the 1920s as xenophobic anxieties over growing immigrant populations sent an Americanization wave over the continent and on to Hawai'i. This was also a time of the burgeoning labor movement in Hawai'i, which ramped up racist fears among haole of the growing Asian immigrant population. This period also saw a post-annexation influx of a new haole population from the continent who could not afford the expensive private schools but did not want their children mixed in with natives and immigrant children (Fuchs 1961, 274–275).

All of these factors led to pressure for the segregation of public schools, increased attention to the Americanization/assimilation of students, and laws against foreign-language schools (Tamura 1993, 45–65). New educational initiatives sought to squeeze all "foreignness" out of students, especially the Japanese (who were mostly Nisei, second-generation children, by that point), stripping them of their cultures and languages. "What Americanizers really wanted was for the Nisei to give undivided loyalty to the United States and discard all vestiges of Japanese culture. They also insisted that the Nisei read, write and speak Standard English, become Christians, obey the law, and be good planta-tion workers" (Tamura 1993, 59).

Fears of retaliation against strict racial segregation led school offi-cials to instead establish a system of English Standard schools in 1924. In this two-tier system, admission to the selective English Standard schools—which received the best teachers, texts, facilities, and equip-ment—was predicated on passing verbal and written English-language tests. Many spoke the language of their parents as well as Hawaiʻi Creole English (HCE), or "pidgin," the hybrid common language of immi-grants constructed through the plantation experience. These students, who did not pass the test, stayed in regular public schools. These bar-riers achieved de facto segregation in the first years, but increasingly Asian students mastered "Standard" English, suppressed HCE accents, and were reluctantly admitted. By 1947, when the English Standard system was abolished, Asians made up 21 percent of English Standard students (Fuchs 1961, 279).

Vestiges of this history were still present in the 1980s, when I was told by a local Japanese teacher at Roosevelt High School that I should be proud to be in a former English Standard school. In the ideology sup-porting this system we can find the origins of the ongoing attacks on HCE within Hawaiʻi public schools. Public education in Hawaiʻi con-tinues to perpetuate colonial injustice, in particular through its failure to Kanaka Maoli students, and I circle back to it in chapter 4.

In today's Hawaiʻi, cane is no longer "king," but tourism and mili-tarism have taken its place with strangleholds on the political econ-omy.[12] Tourism accounts for at least one-third of all jobs and 26 per-cent of state revenue (World Travel & Tourism Council 1999), with the Department of Defense coming in second as the major source of income in the state (Kajihiro 2007, 6). Hawaiian culture was transformed from "sin" to tacky commercialism once tourism began to take off in the decades after annexation. Government and corporate forces have carefully molded Hawai'i into a major tourist destination, simultaneously obscuring its status as the most militarized "state" in the nation. And so, the exploitation of the land for profit and power continues, now in the form of resorts, golf courses, shopping malls, bases, and military training areas. The political economy is such that cost of living is incredibly high, forcing many Kanaka Maoli to leave while middle- and upper-class haoles move in. The haole population is currently the largest in the islands at about 40 percent and on the rise, while Kanaka Maoli make up about 20 percent.

Science also continues to declare its superiority over Hawaiian cultural practices, places, and understandings as demonstrated in current controversies over the University of Hawai'i patenting of taro, the proper reclamation of bones and artifacts from disturbed burial sites, and the astronomical facility atop sacred land on Mauna Kea. Law and politics is seen both as the site of continued colonization (chapter 4 explores the recent lawsuits seeking to end Hawaiian programs and entitlements) and a potential tool for decolonization or deoccupation. The impact of contemporary colonization on Kanaka Maoli is evident in their consistent position at the bottom of all socioeconomic indicators. And yet resistance to colonialism is undying.

## Conclusion

I have tried to touch briefly on some of the key processes that drove haole colonization of Hawai'i. Often colonialism is associated only with European colonies in Africa, South America, and, to a lesser extent, the Pacific, and not with the United States. Disney movies and Western films have warped popular understandings of the bloody conquest of North America. Most Americans think of Puerto Rico, Guam, and Samoa simply as U.S. territories, when we think of them at all. We have vague notions of wars in the Philippines and Mexico. And while increasing numbers of us are troubled by the wars in Iraq and Afghanistan, very rarely are we encouraged to think about those wars in terms of a history of American imperialism.

Indigenous people in all of these places have different understandings of these histories, and different ways of telling these stories than circulate in mainstream American culture. As discussed, language is a key point of contestation in any colonial situation. The ability to continue to define and name places, experiences, and people is central to the life of native cultures and their resistance to colonial forces. Part of that is being able to name the colonizer, and so you have haoles in Hawaiʻi, gringos in Mexico, and Pākehā in Aotearoa (New Zealand). These are all indigenous names for colonial forms of whiteness, and they each carry specific meanings based on their histories.

Hawaiʻi's postcontact history is a complex web of power and resistance that demands much more research and analysis. I urge readers to start with the references I cite and to follow the trails from there, especially seeking out new research by Kanaka Maoli writers. This chapter does not even skim the surface, but hopefully it should now be clear why having some understanding of this colonial history is essential to understanding haole. Next I turn from the history of haole colonization to thinking about how haole as a social construction is produced in relation to native Hawaiian and local identities.

## CHAPTER 2

# "No Ack!"

## What Is Haole, Anyway?

Having established the origins of haole in Hawai'i's colonization, this chapter considers the many different constructions of haole produced by haoles and others from "first contact" to present. As stated earlier, my interest is not so much in trying to define what haole is—as if one definition were possible—as in exploring the different ways it is produced. Haole is dynamic. Not only is it not just one thing, it is also never still—it changes across time, place, and context. How the early missionaries represented themselves differed radically from how Kanaka Maoli constructed them, which differed again from how plantation workers talked about their haole bosses. Understanding haole means thinking about all of these constructs and how they are interrelated with other racial constructions in Hawai'i.

Constructions of the three dominant racial-ethnic groupings in Hawai'i—haoles, locals, and native Hawaiians—are what they are because of each other. Native Hawaiians trace their genealogies back to the time before Cook's arrival. Local identity and culture originated in the plantation system and is an amalgamation of Kanaka Maoli culture with those immigrant groups brought to labor in the sugarcane and pineapple fields. These include Japanese, Chinese, Filipino, Korean, Portuguese, and Samoan immigrants, among others. There could be no local without incorporation of certain elements of Hawaiian culture and resistance to haole hegemony. There could be no white colonizer without a racialized native. Processes of identity formation and racialization (the ways groups come to be understood in racial terms) do not just move in one direction; they move in many directions simultaneously.

My analysis focuses on haole as a colonial/neocolonial form of whiteness situated in Hawai'i, and thus I foreground processes of racialization.

Some literature refers to haole as an ethnic identity. Other authors slide easily between race, ethnicity, and nationality. Different constructions of haole contain elements of all three because they are intrinsically related. I choose to highlight race—race talk, racialization, racial formation, racial production, racial identity, racial politics, racism, and so forth. I focus on active processes of racialization because race is a sociopolitical means of classifying people, not a "natural" biological or scientific fact. Within the context of U.S. imperialism, race has been the foundation for dominant systems of power, the engine driving the imperial machine. By focusing on racial production in Hawai'i, I look at the different deployments of power that produce and reproduce the violent fictions of race, dispossessing some, privileging others, and segregating us from each other and, for those of us with multiple racial identities, often from ourselves.

Theories of racial production contend that racial identities are relational, that the formation of an "us" occurs simultaneously with the formation of a "them." Furthermore, the two processes do not just occur simultaneously, but are also dependent on one another and are mutually constitutive. Whiteness produces itself in opposition to racialized others. It is, so the story goes, what "they" are not. Racialized "others" in turn, produce certain counternarratives or counterdiscourses of whiteness—stories and knowledge about whiteness that runs against dominant (white) ideas. In studying haole, we see how constructions including "savage," "Hawaiian," "Oriental," "Asian," and "local" were, and are, used to mark and patrol the boundaries of haole constructions of haole. At the same time, Hawaiian and local constructions of haole help define the borders of those identities. It is through this interplay and its symbolic and material manifestations that haole gains meaning and significance in multiple, often conflicting, ways.

I begin by exploring haole constructions of haole starting with discoverer and savior, the dominant projections in the first century of haole. I then turn to the more contemporary identities of kama'āina, "Hawaiian at heart," and hapa. Manifest destiny and Christian proselytizing animate the early constructions. A general resistance to being called "haole" and a desire to belong—a yearning to "go native" or become "Hawaiian"—drives the last three. If many haoles could have their way, the word "haole" would be banned as impolite at best, pejorative at worst. One can almost mark one's calendar by the cyclical debate in local media over the use of the word (I analyze this in depth in the next chapter). It is a testament to Hawaiian-local resistance and cultural insistence that the term maintains its usage and salience. The turn to kamaʻāina, Hawaiian at heart, or hapa comes when continental labels including "Caucasian," "Anglo," or "American" fail to stick.

In the second part of the chapter I discuss native Hawaiian and local constructions of haole. Here I draw on Chicana scholar Angie Chabram-Dernersesian's concept of "native constructions of whiteness" and emphasize that understanding any form of whiteness requires looking at it from the perspective of people of color. While there is increasing overlap between them, Hawaiian constructions focus on haole as colonizer, whereas local constructions originate in the experience of haole as plantation owner and oligarch. In Hawaiʻi, these constructions represent forms of racialization-from-below or counternarratives, where a subordinate group's constructions of the dominant group are one form of resistance. In this way we can think of local and Hawaiian constructions of haole as a way of talking back to white supremacy.

Local constructions of haole also emphasize performative haoleness or acting haole, the exhibiting of attitudes and actions that run counter to local and Hawaiian social values. This understanding of haole helps to destabilize essentialized notions that would tie haole solely to white people in Hawaiʻi. The HCE admonishment "no ack" is used to call people out when they are puffing themselves up with claims or actions beyond their abilities or social positioning. One might use this phrase with a local friend who takes on airs of an arrogant haole, or with a haole who insists he is really Hawaiian. I use it as the title for this chapter to highlight the performative, dynamic, contested, and contingent aspects of haole.

Just as haole needs to be analyzed within the institutional processes of colonization, it must also be located in its relationships to other social groupings and racial discourses, which are also central to colonization. This relational analysis makes apparent that haole has always been a contested category, understood in multiple ways by various constituencies. Part of how haole has gained significance is located in how haole is constructed and the consequences of those constructs.

## Haole Constructions of Self

Haole self-productions began with Captain Cook's landing in 1778, the beginning of the influx of haole to Hawaiʻi. These productions were meant for various constituencies at various times: the haole themselves,

the international community, the various funders of haole missionary
work or enterprise, the native Hawaiian population, the American public, and the U.S. government.

### Discoverers and Saviors

When haole first arrived in the islands they talked about how they
"discovered" the islands and everything in them. Then they set about
"saving" things—first Hawaiians, through religion, education, property
ownership, and agriculture; and then Hawai'i, through the utilization
of "underutilized" prized agricultural land and through the fulfillment
of manifest destiny, bringing the fledgling islands under the protective
wing of the American government. These actions presented purpose and
justifications for the being and the doing of haole in Hawai'i.

As explored in chapter 1, the production of haole as "discoverer" was
the first to legitimize haole presence in Hawai'i. It was a critical first
step in the Western imperial project and was managed on the ground
through the issuing of proclamations, the planting of flags, the erecting
of monuments, and the distribution of "gifts." The haole "discovery" of
the islands later became important as the starting point for the dominant version of Hawaiian history: before discovery there was no history,
only "darkness," chaos, and wildness.

Through this story of discovery Kanaka Maoli are neatly dehuman-
ized and folded into the wilderness, disabling any competing claim
to the islands. According to this narrative, it is a tribute to the haole
that Hawai'i was brought into modern times and civilization. Anthropologist Elvi Whittaker demonstrates how many books in the canon
of Hawaiian historiography begin either with Cook's "discovery" or
with the "wild" nature of a volcano erupting from the ocean. She argues
that "these openings tell us more about ourselves than they do about
the world of the Polynesians. . . . When Captain Cook steps ashore, in
actuality or in print, the very act of doing so has become possible only
because of a world view which has 'making discoveries' as a way of making sense of the world" (Whittaker 1986, 8).

The theme of "saving" Hawaiians through religion is strongest in
the period of missionary dominance (roughly 1820–1850) for obvious
reasons. Missionaries were not the only haoles in the islands, but they
were the most influential, and their self-representation as agents of salvation held forth for a number of decades and continues to influence
conceptions of haole today. Many missionaries no doubt truly believed

conversion and westernization were good for Hawaiians. This sense of righteousness was mixed with a good deal of anxiety about being beyond the frontier. As political theorists Phyllis Turnbull and Kathy Ferguson point out, "The colonizers of Hawai'i brought with them both a profound sense of entitlement and a fear of engulfment. . . . Hawai'i's perceived deficiencies provoked both desire (take it, fill it, make it ours) and anxiety (it's different, it's not like us, it's looking back at us). . . . Hawai'i both beckons and disturbs its newcomers" (Turnbull and Ferguson 1997, 99).

There are copious writings (letters, diaries, reports, books) by missionaries about what was, in their minds, their formidable mission. Their writings explicitly express the anxiety Turnbull and Ferguson describe. Of their arrival in the islands in 1820, Reverend Hiram Bingham wrote,

> As we proceeded to shore, the multitudinous, shouting, and almost naked natives . . . exhibited the appalling darkness of the land which we had come to enlighten. Here . . . appeared a just representation of a nation . . . in as deep degradation, ignorance, pollution and destitution as if the riches of salvation . . . had never been provided to enrich and enlighten their souls. (Bingham 1969, 86)

Bingham's intense anxiety only seems to have escalated during his tenure, his project of enlightenment having encountered more resistance than he anticipated. "So darkness and danger have sometimes hung over our young mission, and that infant nation whom we were attempting to guide out of deep embarrassment and gloom, when we seemed ready to be 'swallowed up quick'" (Bingham 1969, 383). Within such an environment, the missionaries frantically tried to reinforce boundaries between themselves and the natives, hoping to keep from being "swallowed up."

Much less concern was expressed for how the salvation project was swallowing up Hawaiians and Hawaiian culture. The exception, expressed by a few women, was concern about the mission's enormous influence and Hawaiians' faith in their civilizing project. Missionary wife Laura Judd wrote in 1828, "We seem to be regarded as but little lower than the angels, and the implicit confidence of these people in our goodness is almost painful" (Judd 1961, 73). The irony, of course, is that it was the Hawaiians, not the missionaries, who bore the pain of "aloha betrayed."[1]

After a couple of decades of effort, many missionaries felt their project of "enlightenment" had failed. This failure they almost exclusively blamed on the Hawaiians. In her article lauding missionary women, historian Patricia Grimshaw sympathetically wrote, "The story of three decades of intercultural contact in Hawai'i, a story of frustration for the mission women and evasion by the Hawaiians, was fraught with considerable tension and unhappiness for both groups of women. Neither side could triumph: by the late 1840s, stalemate was reached" (Grimshaw 1985, 73). There are many interesting aspects to this statement. First, Grimshaw uses the phrase "intercultural contact," which connotes a certain mutual appreciation and respect. There is very little in the writings of missionaries to indicate they considered there was anything "intercultural" at all about the encounter. Second, "evasion" by the Hawaiians is noted, but neither Grimshaw nor other historians have done much to analyze this as a strategic form of resistance and cultural survival.[2] Finally, the passage uses the metaphor of contest or war—there was "stalemate," neither could "triumph"—which seems to belie the idea of intercultural exchange.

As indicated in chapter 1, in the 1840s haole discourse began to shift from being dominated by conversion to more secular forms of saving the Hawaiians. This shift was tied to the increasing importance of the islands in international trade and military strategy. As world powers began to pay more attention to Hawai'i and Hawai'i formed diplomatic relations with a number of nations, missionary families began to think of the islands as a permanent residence rather than just a temporary outpost. As they began building their lives in the islands, they began to think about schools for their children (Punahou School was established in 1841), government, property, and economic opportunity. Missionary attitudes seemed to suggest that if Hawaiians could not be made to see that conversion would save them, surely they could be convinced of the need for civilizing themselves through education, property ownership, agriculture, and democratic government. Thus efforts in education were redoubled, a constitutional monarchy was established, the Māhele converted 'āina into property, and Hawaiians were encouraged to labor in capitalist agriculture.

In 1853 the American Board of Commissioners for Foreign Missions (ABCFM) dissolved its mission in Hawai'i, declaring the islands sufficiently Christianized to have their own home mission. The missionaries were effectively cut loose, officially encouraged to become Hawaiian citizens and purchase property (Wilson 2000, 533). By this point, the dominant thinking was that if the Hawaiians were still having trouble, it was certainly through no fault of the missionaries, who, after all, had spent decades on conversion, education, and all forms of civilizing efforts.

As discussed in chapter 1, the discourse of saving Hawai'i becomes increasingly tied to a rhetoric characterizing the Hawaiian monarchy as corrupt, ineffective, and tyrannical. This characterization hits a viciously racist, sexist, and demeaning climax with the campaign to defame Queen Lili'uokalani in the years before and after the overthrow of the Hawaiian monarchy. For example, missionary son Reverend Sereno Bishop charged the queen with having no royal heredity, being "African" in appearance, and not being respected by her people (Kualapai 2005, 45). These negative representations of the queen and other ali'i enabled a glorification of American (read: haole) Hawai'i. A senior member of the *Pacific Commercial Advertiser* staff printed an opinion of many haoles in 1900: "In spite of the large number of Hawaiians and Orientals on these islands this is essentially an American community. White men, chiefly Americans, have built it up from nothing and have made it one of the most prosperous and modern and progressive places in the world" (as quoted in Basson 2005, 592). It logically followed that, having saved the islands and converted them into prosperous and modern places, the haole was not going to let recalcitrant natives squander all that had been gained.

And so it was not difficult for the haole conspirators against the queen to narrate themselves as revolutionaries throwing off the yoke of royal despotism. That is the representation most supported by haole historians through the decades.[3] Not surprisingly, Thurston Twigg-Smith—grandson of Lorrin Thurston, a key architect of the overthrow—strongly promotes this view in his book *Hawaiian Sovereignty: Do the Facts Matter?*: "At the time of the Revolution, following the time-honored international practice of revolt as a last-ditch means for people to change their governments, control of the Islands was seized from the Queen by a volunteer army of Hawai'i residents" (Twigg-Smith 1998, 7–8). Twigg-Smith, and Thurston before him, drew easy analogies between the Hawai'i coup and the American Revolution. Yet Tom Coffman writes, "The Committee of Annexation . . . represented as little as

2 percent of the population, and never more than 4 or 5 percent. This was what Thurston described as the popular revolution that became the stock subject of so much written history" (Coffman 1998, 124).

Eric Love, a scholar of the annexation of Hawai'i and the Philippines, asserts that Hawai'i was annexed for the sake of the haoles. While Love overstates his argument by not considering the other factors motivating Congress (Hawai'i's strategic military location, for example), race and racial politics did play a significant role in the annexation debate.[4] Haole annexationists argued that the hard work they had done civilizing the islands was threatened by the incompetence of the monarchy, and then the royalists after the overthrow, and a gathering "oriental menace" in the East.

The "oriental menace" has become more prominent in contemporary arguments justifying the overthrow. Haoles (and haolified non-Japanese locals) often tout the line of "better America than Japan," following the inevitability theory of Hawai'i's colonization. One such letter in the *Honolulu Weekly* states, "Hawai'i was destined to be taken over by some greater power. As for how the Hawaiians would have fared under Japanese occupation, there are numerous examples. . . . [P]opulations were subjected to the horrors of torture, rape, enslavement and execution" (Lee 2003). The U.S., by contrast, is supposed to be understood as a benevolent occupier.

Love notes that when Lorrin Thurston went to lobby Congress in 1897, he did all he could to quell fears of embracing such a nonwhite territory by representing Hawai'i as the white child of Uncle Sam. He opportunistically counted Portuguese as white to inflate those numbers (as discussed later in this chapter, Portuguese are not considered haole, but part of the local) and claimed that the Chinese would leave if Hawai'i were annexed (Love 1997, 157–163). A year later, when the Senate Foreign Relations Committee met to consider an annexation resolution, it was clear Thurston's words had hit their mark. In their report calling for annexation, the committee wrote, "The really distinctive feature of [Hawaiian] society is that it is American in all its traits and habits" (as quoted in Love 1997, 175).

The idea of a march of progress in Hawai'i led by the capable haole—from darkness and chaos to Christianity, education, capitalism, and, finally, inevitable Americanization—was successfully mobilized by the annexationists. In 1893 missionary son Samuel Chapman Armstrong wrote it was commonly accepted that "the conquest by American missionaries of the Hawaiian Islands for a degree of Christian civilization gives the United State both a claim and an obligation in the matter—a claim to be considered first in the final disposition of that country, and an obligation to save the decency and civilization in that utterly broken-down monarchy" (as quoted in Love 1997, 130). Saving Hawai'i from a "broken-down" government was one thing; incorporating it into the motherland was quite another. To become a state, Hawai'i would again have to be represented as white as possible. "Annexation made the triumph of white values and ideology through 'Americanization' a formal necessity if the new territory was ever to achieve statehood" (Bell 1984, 36). And so the haole elite recognized the need to flex their dominance for all to see. In testimony before Congress in 1921, the secretary of the powerful Hawaiian Sugar Planters Association reported, "The Territory of Hawaii is now and is going to be American; it is going to remain American under any condition and we are going to control the situation out there. The white race, the white people, the Americans in Hawaii are going to dominate and will continue to dominate—there is no question about it" (as quoted in Okamura 1998, 272).

Having constructed themselves as the clear choice for political leadership, haoles continued to consolidate their political power after annexation. They formed alliances with native Hawaiians against the growing population of Asian immigrants, who they feared would seize power. Conveniently for the haole power brokers, anti-Asian racism and discrimination were at their height nationally, and (although as a territory, now bound to uphold the nettlesome U.S. doctrine of equal rights) Asian immigrants were barred from naturalization by acts of Congress. It was, in fact, this particularly anti-Asian racism that scholars credit in prolonging Hawai'i's territorial period. Roger Bell, in his book on statehood, contends, "The racial and political complexion of Hawaii's voters, and the anticipated impact they would have on the fortunes of conservative and racially sensitive factions of Congress, were the central reasons why it was for so long denied equality as a state" (Bell 1984, 6).[5]

### Mutual Constitution of Haole

The period between annexation and statehood offers a good illustration of the processes through which haole was constructed relationally. Haole constructions of self were successful to the extent that they were coupled with the racialization of others in Hawai'i. Hawai'i scholar J. Kēhaulani Kauanui lays out how the racialization of Kanaka Maoli was part of haole constructions of haole. She notes that on the continent, early constructions of whiteness are established in the triangulation of Indian/Black/white, while in Hawai'i, Hawaiian/Asian/white formed a similar triangulation (Kauanui 2000, 28). Using work by legal theorist Cheryl Harris, Kauanui demonstrates that whiteness is a form of property in that whiteness confers on its owners rights of disposition, use and enjoyment, reputation and status, and exclusion. Harris makes the point that these functions of whiteness have meaning and value only because they are denied to others (Harris 1993, 1744). In other words, they are part of the defining and patrolling of racial borders. There would be no whiteness if there were no others who are excluded from the privileges of whiteness. In Hawai'i, there would be no haole without native Hawaiians and locals.

Kauanui adds "the right to include" to Harris' list and describes the politics of assimilation of native peoples (Kauanui 2000, 54). She shows how Hawaiians, like Native Americans, could be accepted as white if their blood was "diluted" enough and their performance assimilated enough (what counts as enough is a moving target). Much more can be gained by subsuming natives (not the least of which are property and assumed absolution from the "sins" of colonization) than continuing to lock them out. And so the 1921 Hawaiian Homes Commission Act launched government efforts at the rehabilitation and assimilation of Hawaiians: "Selective assimilation has played as much a role in the formation of whiteness as has exclusion. For American Indians and Hawaiians, the legacies of inclusion have worked against collective assertions of legal subjectivity by conferring the franchise rather than sovereign recognition" (Kauanui 2000, 78).

By contrast, Asians have historically been seen as much more threatening in their otherness, making them forever foreign and suspect, even when assimilated. There is a well-documented history of this in Hawai'i that includes suppression of language, denial of citizenship, and many other forms of discrimination (Tamura 1993, Odo 2004). By playing Asians against Hawaiians, and "native" Hawaiians against "part" Hawaiians, haoles managed the borders of haole, granting and denying access. Part of what makes haole haole is just these processes of mutual constitution.

*Hawaiian, Kama'āina, "Hawaiian at Heart," and Hapa*

Appropriation (taking as one's own something of another's, especially with regard to culture), the twin to assimilation and inclusion, plays an equally strong role in processes of racialization. The blatant colonial assertion by haole that they are Hawaiian seems to have first appeared in the period around the overthrow, and some still assert it today. The appropriation of kama'āina, the creation of "Hawaiian at heart," and the wiggle toward hapa are some common contemporary responses to being named haole. These claims to being anything but haole lay bare desperate longing to escape haole and become naturalized by going native.

In 1894, in testimony supporting the overthrow, Albert F. Judd, missionary son and chief justice of the Republic's Supreme Court, stated, "I am a Hawaiian. . . . I was born in this country. I love this country. It is my country" (Kualapai 2005, 39–40). While we might understand this as a claim to Hawaiian citizenship (as opposed to indigeneity), which many haole had prior to the overthrow, the anxious repetition with which it is made should give us pause. Judd's purpose was to set up a logic whereby his actions and desires were seen as patriotic. He was, in his view, part of a revolutionary government selflessly acting on behalf of Hawai'i. Twigg-Smith follows suit a century later, claiming five generations of missionary blood make him Hawaiian, while using the technology of blood quantum to diminish ten generations of native Hawaiian ancestry by claiming dilution: "As a fifth-generation resident, this writer considers himself every bit as much a 'Hawaiian' as anyone whose family roots here can be traced back ten generations but who might at this distance from his native ancestor possess only one-thirty-second Hawaiian blood" (Twigg-Smith 1998, 4–5).

Houston Wood explores the processes by which missionaries and haole elite began appropriating "kama'āina" and using it as a badge of belonging. Kama'āina is a Kanaka Maoli word that literally translates to "land child" and means "native-born, one born in a place, host" (Pukui and Elbert 1986, 124). Those haole originally claiming kama'āina status were a select group largely from New England with political and economic power and close association with the ali'i through intermarriage. They sought to distinguish and separate themselves from haole newcomers and those of lower social status. While the term is still used by some in this way, haole commoners democratized it, adopting the label for those who had been in the islands for at least seven years or who were born in the islands: "Kama'āina was thus transformed from a concept denoting Native-born into a term meaning 'island-born,' or even merely 'well-acquainted with the islands.' By adopting a Native word

44CHAPTER 2

to describe themselves, Euroamericans obscured both their origins and the devastating effects their presence was having on the Native-born" (Wood 1999, 41). Further appropriation has taken place, and the term is now sometimes used to refer to all residents, regardless of race or class. This broad application has proven very successful as a marketing tool by conferring both belonging and status on nonnative residents—for example, kamaʻāina vacation packages, entrance fees, and supermarket cards.

"Hawaiian at heart" has more potentially insidious meanings. Wood suggests that this phrase began to circulate with the boom in tourism that followed statehood. It was a way of ensuring haole visitors could have the exotic "Hawaiian experience" without staying years to earn the kamaʻāina badge (Wood 1999, 48–49). You could be "Hawaiian at heart" by simply wading in the ocean and eating some kalua pig at a commercial lūau.

The "Hawaiian at heart" label has come to be used by haole residents in similar fashion to kamaʻāina, to assert belonging and long-term residence while additionally indicating an affinity for, or knowledge of, Hawaiian culture. In some New Age circles, it parallels the phenomenon of white people declaring Native American ancestry—which, given five hundred years of colonization, is harder to trace.[6] In her research, political scientist Kelly Kraemer found that Hawaiians were generally skeptical of anyone proclaiming her or himself "Hawaiian at heart." One interviewee wonders, "What happened to *their* heart?" Another states, "When we meet a non-native who wants to be supportive we kind of hold our breath and hope that this isn't gonna be another burden to us or another idiot who thinks they wanna be Hawaiian. . . . We all should celebrate our own history" (as quoted in Kraemer 2000, 362).

While Kraemer's interviewees display a certain level of humor and tolerance, the claim can open deep scars, especially when coupled with an arrogance about knowing and practicing Hawaiian culture. Native Hawaiian scholar Lisa Kahaleole Hall writes,

> "Hawaiians at heart" assume that knowing and appreciating Hawaiian culture is enough to transform them into being Hawaiian. Indeed, some have gone so far as to claim that they are more Hawaiian than actual Hawaiians, because they have greater cultural or language knowledge. [B]ut . . . all contemporary Hawaiians come from a past where our parents',

grandparents', or great-grandparents' use of Hawaiian language and culture was forbidden, legislated against, brutally
punished, or a combination of these. Non-Hawaiians without
this history do not carry a legacy of internalized fear, shame and
anger to impede their study, nor do they feel guilt about this
history. (Hall 2005, 410–411)

Hall goes on to take issue with those who use claims of Hawaiianness
to make money by selling spiritual retreats and experiences. This phenomenon of appropriating and marketing indigenous culture, often by
representing oneself as more native than the natives, is very familiar to
Native Americans who worry about a scourge of "white shamans and
plastic medicine men."[7]

Native scholar Eva Marie Garroutte studied the issue of self-iden-
tified Native Americans and the phenomenon of "ethnic switching,"
or being a "born-again Indian." Her native respondents gave mixed
responses. Some saw it as outright appropriation: "How do you get to
be the sort of victor who can claim to be the vanquished also?" Others want to be more inclusive: "One of the fundamental human rights
of individuals and groups includes the right to self-identification and
self-definition" (as quoted in Garroutte 2003, 55 and 94). A number of
Native American scholars see dangers in heavily policing native identity
boundaries. They argue that not all ethnic switching is done for personal gain. It can also allow for "the introduction of new resources into
tribal communities—resources ranging from the professional, intellectual, and financial, to the cultural, emotional, and spiritual" (Garroutte
2003, 97).

Kraemer's Kanaka Maoli interviewees also note that the designa-
tion of "Hawaiian at heart" has very different meaning when offered by a
Hawaiian rather than as self-declared. It can be used by one Hawaiian to
another to communicate, "She's okay, she gets it." Rona Tamiko Halualani discusses the reappropriation of "Hawaiian at heart" by diasporic
Hawaiians in their Aloha Clubs as a way to allow for membership of
non-Hawaiian friends and family:

A "Hawaiian at heart" identity position is invoked among
mainland Hawaiians as a localized adjustment to a different
social fabric of the mainland. It works on one level as a form
of public outreach through which community membership

boundaries are adapted, and yet, internally, it remains within
a differentiating hierarchy of Hawaiian identity. . . . [S]everal
members cast "Hawaiians at heart" as friends but not "true/
authentic *kanaka*." (Halualani 2002, 200)

"Hapa" is a relative newcomer to the block of haole self-identifi-
cations. Originally meaning "of mixed blood" in Hawaiian (Pukui and
Elbert 1986, 58), it is more commonly understood in HCE as the short
form of "hapa haole," meaning half or part haole. My anecdotal experience in Hawai'i is that it is often invoked by a haole parent about his
or her child, conceivably as a way to claim belonging for and through
that child. Conversely, it can be used by locals to indicate that a child
has a haole parent. Its popularity, especially among young people—
hapa clubs, hapa music, and hapa literature—is another indication of
the powerful desire to be something other than haole.

A University of Hawai'i professor shared a relevant story about her
teenage son. One day he told her that he was hapa, and when she asked
how, he said because she was haole and his dad was Israeli. He was cre-
atively trying to find an out for himself, like so many haole youth. I can
only guess that when he proclaimed his "hapaness" to his local friends,
he found that whiteness is not parsed in the islands in the same ways it
is on the continent.[8]

Hapa identity is often romanticized by haoles and held out as an
indicator of racial harmony, a symbol of island-style colorblind ideology.
This narrative tends to ignore historical and continuing haole dominance by pretending all is well in paradise. Curt Sanburn, former editor
of the popular *Honolulu Weekly,* ends a lament about feeling like an "Ur-
haole" growing up by offering hapa identity as the hope for the future:
"I am optimistic that our children, the statistically large golden generation coming up behind us, will eventually dissolve most of the real and
imagined racial divisions that trouble our politics" (Sanburn 1998). This
story, of interracial coupling as the agent for "dissolving" the harms and
injustices of colonialism and white supremacy, is undoubtedly familiar.
I return to this in my discussion of the racial harmony discourse in the
next chapter.

In the last decade "hapa" has made a splash on the continent, especially among young Asian Americans who have retranslated it yet again.
For them the featured identity is Asian, so that while it usually means
half Asian and half white, it can mean half Asian and half something

else, or simply mixed Asian with other racial identities (it is not used in this way in Hawai'i since here the same group will identify as local or by a particular Asian ancestry). It is probable that the increasing popularity of contemporary Hawaiian music on the continent and the persistent desire to go native are influencing factors in this appropriation.

## Native Hawaiian and Local Constructions of Haole

Chicana scholar Angie Chabram-Dernersesian points out that studies of whiteness often focus only on dominant white identities, which leads to static, essentialized notions of whiteness. These include ideas about whiteness as an unmarked category, an invisible center, and a naturalized identity. While many white people on the continent may experience whiteness in this way, it is certainly not universally understood in these terms, especially in communities of color. Hawai'i is an obvious case in point, as discussed in my introduction. Not enough attention has been paid in whiteness studies to the ways people of color construct whiteness, despite the richness of that literature. Chabram-Dernersesian finds that counterdiscourses of whiteness within the Chicana/o community serve multiple purposes. They help Chicanas/os navigate and name social relations, negotiate a political identity (Chicana/o), think about other forms of oppression, and imagine different social locations for self and others (Chabram-Dernersesian 1999, 111).

I believe counterdiscourses of haole play similar roles for Kanaka Maoli and locals, which could be part of the reason why many are angered by suggestions that the term be banned. It is not just that "haole" is a legitimate Hawaiian and HCE word; more important, it is an extremely useful *political* word.[9] "Haole" does not simply translate to "white" or "Caucasian," as many haoles would like to suggest, because it carries with it a specific legacy of colonization. No one says, "Eh, Caucasian," because that has no meaning in the islands. Clearly, counterdiscourses of haole help in the navigation of social relations, the naming of colonial processes, and the exposing of haole hegemony. It is also useful to think about the ways Hawaiian and local counterdiscourses of haole allow for the negotiation of Kanaka Maoli and local political identities.

Chabram-Dernersesian writes about how Chicana/o counterdiscourses of whiteness deterritorialize and bracket whiteness—they move whiteness from the center of the political geography to the sidelines. Local and native Hawaiian counterdiscourses of haole involve similar elements of deterritorializing and bracketing in that they mark haole, calling it into question and obstructing its efforts at naturalization. The simple phrase "Eh, haole" can do that work. Local and native Hawaiian counter-discourses are now quite interrelated, but understanding them more fully requires looking at their evolutions. Kanaka Maoli experience with, and therefore discourse about, haole has a longer history than that of the local and is founded in colonialism. The relationship between the local and the haole began in sugar and pineapple plantations decades later.

### Native Hawaiian Constructions of Haole

The early Kanaka Maoli understanding of the haole is the subject of much debate and an area requiring much more research. Hawaiian-language primary sources have barely been tapped for what they might yield on the subject, limiting the current discussion to English-language sources. Once these sources are researched, much of what we currently understand about Hawaiian historiography will inevitably change, including what we know about early Hawaiian constructions of haole.

The breadth of the contemporary arguments run from whether Kanaka Maoli believed Captain Cook was a god, to why the ali'i enlisted haole as leaders and advisers, to why the ali'i easily accepted Christianity and Western law. Clearly, just as haole constructions of themselves changed, so too did Kanaka Maoli constructions of themselves and of haole—many of which were undoubtedly quite different than the image the haole was presenting (or in the case of contemporary debates, re-presenting).

Anthropologists have engaged in considerable debate over whether or not Captain Cook was misrecognized as the Hawaiian god Lono. The notion of Cook as a god has been perpetuated in popular discourse as well. Lydia K. Kualapai writes, "The Eurocentric myth of preliterate natives venerating the awesome white man as a god has been central to the colonial discourse about Hawai'i since the early nineteenth century" (Kualapai 2001, 18). The scaffolding provided by this narrative supports the subsequent positionings by haole discussed earlier. If the natives believed the haole to be a god once, surely the haole could be savior of the people, the land, the government, and the territory. Kualapai and others pay attention to a more nuanced understanding of traditional Kanaka Maoli politics and cosmology. They ask questions about nonnative scholars' singular focus on studying natives, the desire to fix one single mind-set on Hawaiians at the time, and how ali'i actions may have been prompted by political necessity.[10]

Political necessity also seems to be a key to understanding aliʻi willingness to rely on haole as advisers and to convert to Christianity and Western law. Rather than adopting a foreign ideology of racial hierarchy or seeing godlike qualities in the haole, it is certainly equally probable that the aliʻi were assessing their rapidly changing world and making strategic judgments influenced by crisis, power, and desire. As discussed in chapter 1, Hawaiians were dying at a rate of nine out of ten, causing a cultural crisis far beyond any they had ever experienced. This at the same time haole power was mounting. Jonathan K. Osorio submits, "It is even conceivable that the chiefs saw their role in very traditional ways. If it was haole power that mattered in the world now, then it was up to the Aliʻi to mediate that power to the rest of the community in the same way that the sacred chiefs had once mediated the power of Kū and Lono" (Osorio 2002, 38).

As is often the case, those with less power, and alternate desires, made different assessments of the haole (of course, as Osorio just pointed out, they also had less responsibility vis-à-vis the haole). As Samuel M. Kamakau contended at the time (printed in 1992), and Jonathan K. Osorio (2002) and Sally Engle Merry (2000) contend today, the makaʻāinana were much more skeptical of and resistant to haole leadership and the imposition of Western law than were many of the aliʻi. Consider this passage from Kamakau about the conversion to Western law:

> The truth was, they were laws to change the old laws of the natives of the land and cause them to lick ti leaves like the dogs and gnaw bones thrown at the feet of strangers, while the strangers became their lords, and the hands and voices of strangers were raised over those of the native race. The commoners knew this and one and all expressed their disapproval and asked the king not to place foreigners in the offices of government lest the native race become a footstool for the foreigners. (Kamakau 1992, 339)

If, in the first century after contact, the aliʻi tried to mediate haole power and the makaʻāinana tried to resist it, Kanaka Maoli across the board saw the haole as increasingly gaining power and significance. In the above citations, Kamakau wrote of "strangers becoming lords" and Osorio speculates that aliʻi felt "it was haole power that mattered in the world now." I think it is safe to say that in the diversity of early native constructions of haole, the common thread was anxiety over growing haole power. It is interesting that anxiety seemed to be the key element to both early Hawaiian and haole constructions of haole. Haole anxiety over being engulfed by "the savage" caused larger-than-life self-representations. Native anxiety over these grandiose haole self-representations and their violent consequences prompted their resentment and caution.

After over two centuries of trying to understand, approximate, mitigate, and resist haole power, Hawaiians are experts on the subject. Kanaka Maoli discourses of haole share a good deal with local discourses, but with a colonial difference. Of all Hawai'i's diverse populations, the indigenous population is consistently the worst off. As I will discuss further in chapter 4, Kanaka Maoli have the highest unemployment, lowest life expectancy, highest alcohol and drug problems, disproportionately high welfare representation, disproportionately high incarceration, disproportionately low educational achievement, the highest rate of hypertension and diabetes, and so forth (State of Hawai'i Department of Business 2006). Contemporary native Hawaiian constructions of haole are intrinsically tied to the experience of these conditions—the present-day manifestations of colonization—and the resistance to them. Haoles are "interlopers," colonizers, and occupiers who have succeeded in making Hawaiians "strangers in our own land" (Trask 2002a, 256). In *From a Native Daughter,* Haunani-Kay Trask writes,

> We have been occupied by a colonial power whose every law, policy, cultural institution, and collective behavior entrench foreign ways of life in our land and on our people. From the banning of our language and the theft of our sovereignty to forcible territorial incorporation in 1959 as a state of the United States, we have lived as a subordinated Native people in our ancestral home. (Trask 1993, 23)

These constructions can fix haole and Kanaka Maoli as polar opposites instead of recognizing their interrelation, contradictions, contingency, and complexity. Yet most Hawaiian nationalists complicate this simplistic us-versus-them setup by finding space for haole allies. Trask writes that there are "haole exceptions" who have proven themselves in years of struggle. "*Haole* who honestly support us, do so without loud pronouncements about how *they* feel what *we* feel or how they *know* just what we *mean*. Moreover, they readily acknowledge our leadership" (Trask 1993, 251). On the question of allies, Kekuni Blaisdell, who has a Japanese hānai (similar to adoption but informal) son, says, "Those who share [Kanaka Maoli] values are welcome. We hānai you if you want to live our way" (Blaisdell 2003). Lilikalā Kameʻeleihiwa says that the old saying about allies used to be "If you can cook, you can stay," and the new maxim should be "If you love and support us, you can stay" (Kameʻeleihiwa and Spivak 2003). These sentiments echo some of the Native American views on "ethnic switching" discussed earlier.

### Local Constructions of Haole

If haole-Hawaiian relations find their basis in colonization, haole-local relations were molded in Hawaiʻi's plantations, where the local itself had its beginnings. The past three decades have seen an explosion of local literature, arts, and cultural studies. Within local cultural studies, two of the strongest debates revolve around origins and definitions of local and what the relationship should be between the local and Hawaiian sovereignty politics. HCE, local humor, and local claims to place all help decenter and question haole authority at the same time that they highlight the dynamic nature of local identity.

The processes of racialization involved in the plantation system have been well documented.[11] The main distinction to be upheld through these systems was a class division between haoles and labor (the foundation of the local), but the haole deployed a divide-and-conquer strategy to keep labor from consolidating (a strategy that began to crack with a big strike in 1920 and was broken in the decades after by interracial solidarity).[12] Tactics included physical and social segregation, the pitting of racial/ethnic groups against one another, discriminatory laws and contracts, physical violence and coercion, and a racist ideology. Ronald Takaki wrote, "As planters imported workers to meet their labor needs in the nineteenth century, they created a racially stratified labor structure based on an ideology of white supremacy" (Takaki 1983, 76). This structure was made manifest in the physical layout of the plantation.

> Indeed the physical organization of plantation housing reflected, as well as reinforced, a social hierarchy. The manager lived in a mansion with spacious verandas and white columns overlooking the plantation; his foremen and technical employees were

housed in "handsome bungalow cottages." . . . [W]orkers of
different nationalities were usually housed in separate buildings or camps. (Takaki 1983, 93)

This segregation carried over beyond the plantation, with haoles
establishing their own institutions (schools, clubs, newspapers, social
and business networks) and neighborhoods,[13] and intermixing as little as possible with the new immigrant populations. It is exactly this
segregation that produced the conditions giving rise to local culture,
language, and politics. Local scholar Louise Kubo writes, "While the
haole plantation owners/managers no doubt sought to keep the great
unwashed masses at a safe distance, this separation had the concomitant
effect of keeping the haoles away from the immigrants and shielding
them from haole cultural dominance, including language" (Kubo 1997,
10). Kubo goes on to discuss the emergence of HCE and other elements
of local culture as significant elements of local identity.

The question of the origin of the local involves the local construction of haole, since they are relational. Further, some argue that the
local emerged as an identity of resistance, as a counterstance to haole,
and thus is much more about politics than culture. In this view, the
foundational representation of the haole is as the greedy plantation
owner. Local scholar Jonathan Okamura (1998) is the strongest propo-
nent of this view. Okamura and those who emphasize local as resistant
also tend to construct haole fairly rigidly. Haole is the anti-local, everything the local is not. Such constructions can obscure haole-Hawaiian
relations and colonization through a singular focus on a haole-local
binary.

One continental scholar has even placed the origins of haole, not
just local, in the plantation. Evelyn Nakano Glenn writes, "The consolidation of haole as a racial category occurred with the development
of the plantation and the need for the small proprietorial and manage-
rial class to distinguish itself from workers" (Glenn 2002, 207). Such a
view privileges a class analysis at the expense of other axes of power and
thus erases a hundred years of haole colonization forged via the multiple
modes discussed in the previous chapter. It should be clear by now that
haole began consolidating itself as a racial category as soon as Cook set
foot on the beach. While the plantation was undoubtedly the origin of
the local's haole, as I have shown, it was certainly not the origin of the
Hawaiian's haole, or haoles' depiction of themselves as a group.

Another group of local scholars argues that local culture and identity are not simply reactions to the haole. For them, many elements of the local have little if anything to do with haole. This group is divided between those who want to promote the local as a model of multicultural harmony (Grant and Ogawa 1993, Takaki 1983) and those who are unwilling to smooth over the disharmony and messiness within the local (Kubo 1997, Fujikane 2000, Chang 1995, Saranillio 2008). The multiculturalists tend to deemphasize the negative aspects of haole. Haole is just one of many groups of people living in racial harmony in Hawai'i.

Those who think more critically about the local see identities as much more complicated, intersected, and conflicted. They tend to recognize the history of colonialism as driven by the haole, but not without the complicity of some segments of the local, particularly local Japanese. Also for them, some locals can be as haole as the most haole of haoles. They recognize the relational, contingent character of identity production and see the current triangulation of social identities as Kanaka Maoli/local/haole. Heated debates rage regarding the firmness and the elasticity of the borders between these identities.

One of the things visitors and scholars frequently note is the extent to which people in Hawai'i openly categorize each other by race. This makes many "mainlanders" uncomfortable, since they are used to a culture that politely pretends to be colorblind. One of the mainstays of local culture is the way it marks, stereotypes, and pokes fun at the different groups in the islands. Haole is far from exempt. Hawai'i's comedians rely heavily on this culture of racial/ethnic humor. Those who take offense, often a marker of uptight haoleness, are met with the challenge, "Wat, no can take one joke?" Kubo ties local humor to the cultural importance of humility (often reinforced by teasing): "Local humor acts to keep us from thinking too much of ourselves. . . . One of the ways it does this is by calling attention to race and ethnicity. It takes that which has been a tool of oppression, of public and private shame and humiliation, and through caricature and parody transforms it into a source of humor" (Kubo 1997, 58).

In HCE, haole definitely is as much about how one acts as anything else. In *Pidgin to Da Max,* an early humorous reference on HCE, haole is defined as "Caucasian, or someone who acts like one." The use of "Caucasian" here is further evidence of haole as nonlocal since the book's definitions are given in (often exaggerated) "Standard" English, while the examples are in HCE. The very next listing is "Haolefied: Just like a haole. *"George went mainlan' an' he wen come back so haolefied I hahdly knew heem!"*(Simonson 1981).

While there are all sorts of constructions of haole in contemporary local culture, for the most part they are variations on a theme, differing in degree. Haole in local discourse is generally arrogant, aggressive, ignorant of island cultures and histories, greedy, loud, and rude. The upper-class character that used to be implicit in haole has largely fallen away as haole has become more class stratified, although one's degree of haoleness still often correlates with class. Haole often wishes it were elsewhere (usually somewhere less "provincial" and always more white); it will not or cannot adapt to the island environment and culture.

The deterritorializing or decentering of haole within local discourse is familiar to those who have spent time in the islands. A self-made bumper sticker on a customized pickup truck I observed one day read, "Locals Only: We Grew Here, U Flew Here." While the "locals only" phrase is common, the second part more specifically does the work of marking haole (and to a lesser extent nonlocal people of color) as outside, neither legitimate in, nor natural to, Hawai'i. At the same time, it counters white ethnocentrism by suggesting that while locals proved their strength and commitment by "growing" here, haoles came by plane, taking the easy route to Hawai'i.

An incident in a class at the University of Hawai'i provides an extremely useful parsing of haole. A haole student from California on a one-year exchange program ended up in one of my classes. Almost from day one she expressed irritation at being called out as a haole. She complained in the usual continental style that it was rude and discriminatory for others to affix this label to her. After a few weeks of listening to this student, our haole professor spoke from her fifty-plus years of experience in Hawai'i. Phyllis Turnbull instructed the student: "You have three choices. You can be a haole, a dumb haole, or a dumb fucking haole. It's up to you." This description stuck with me as it captures the essence of local constructions of haole.

Turnbull later elaborated that at the first level, "haole" is simply a descriptor, used as any racial descriptor is used in Hawai'i. The level of "dumb haole" involves a sociocultural not noticing, such as not bringing food to a gathering, or kicking sand on someone as you run past.[14] Locals will tolerate a certain amount of this behavior, especially in newcomers, and stereotypes are often used to mark and defuse it. Louise Kubo writes,

> Stereotypes . . . help grease the wheels of interethnic interaction. They remind us that others' behavior cannot be judged through our own specific ethnic/cultural lenses. "Haole 'as why," depersonalizes and defuses behavior that might otherwise be interpreted as rude within one's own cultural standards. This understanding of behavior as determined by culture and the recognition of variation between cultures creates space, a kind of leeway, in which cross-cultural interactions can take place. (Kubo 1997, 58)

But "dumb fucking haoles" rarely go unchallenged. They cross the line from relatively benign ignorance to belligerent disrespect for people and place.

The case of Portuguese immigrants illuminates the way racialization often creates its own paradoxes and contradictions and is therefore inherently unstable. The haole elite manipulated Portuguese racialization to fit their various needs. Brought to work on the plantations, the Portuguese were often put in position as lunas (field bosses), bridging the ever-widening distance between haole managers and workers. They were given this middle position in the racial plantation hierarchy due to their assumed "racial closeness" to the haole.

> Their hulking size in comparison to the Asians, their European language base, and their Caucasian features associated them with the power elite, while their dark complexions and non-Anglo customs linked them to the working immigrant class. . . . While the Anglo remained separate and aloof from the workers, assuming a status accorded racially based deference symbolized in their sometimes being known as "Father" and "Mother" to the workers, the Portuguese *luna* took the brunt of hostility, resentment, and rebellion. (Grant and Ogawa 1993, 144)

The Portuguese luna enjoyed perks to maintain their loyalty to the haole manager, but they were never considered haole—except when it suited the elite, such as when Thurston wanted to represent Hawai'i as essentially white and therefore included them in the demographic count. Evidence of the precarious position of the Portuguese is also found in their disenfranchisement following the overthrow. In his letter seeking advice on the construction of a new constitution for the illegal Republic, Sanford Dole singled out "natives and Portuguese" for disenfranchisement because he felt they were "ignorant of the principles of government" (Dole as quoted in Castle 1981, 27).

In processes similar to those involved in the racialization of native Hawaiians, Portuguese were partially included at times and wholly excluded at others. The borders of haole, local, and Hawaiian were continually reworked around, and with, them. In an article about race relations in Hawai'i during World War II, Beth Bailey and David Farber write,

> "Caucasian" meant little to island residents. The more important category in Hawaii was "haole" (literally "stranger"), a term with a complicated history that by 1940 designated the relatively affluent whites of Northern European ancestry. Members of ethnic groups that had come to Hawaii to do plantation work, no matter how light-skinned, were not considered haoles. Thus Caucasian Portuguese and Puerto Ricans were not haoles (and were listed in census data as "other Caucasians"). Haoles made up less than 15% of the islands' population. The term "local" often designated the rest of the islands' peoples. (Bailey and Farber 1993, 818–819)

Portuguese or Puerto Ricans who take the initiative on their own to try to pass as haole in the islands are quickly exposed with the public accusation, "No ack!" In some ways this might be seen as the local policing its borders, but in other ways it is consistent with the local cultural ethic of humility, since to act haole is to act with hubris.

## Conclusion

Hawai'i could use more scholarship on local constructions of haole that moves beyond the polarized debate over whether local is simply the flip side of haole. Clearly the relationship is more complex. One starting point could be Chabram-Dernersesian's idea that counterdiscourses of whiteness serve multiple purposes in nonwhite communities. How do the counterdiscourses of haole in Kanaka Maoli and local communities serve those communities? How does the fluidity of Hawaiian and local constructions of haole—colonizer, ally, oppressor, anyone acting superior—help those communities navigate a sea of social and political relations, a sea where the aggressive, insatiable haole tsunami often looms large?

Going back to the chapter title, what is haole anyway at the end of all of this? Haole is all of these constructions produced by haoles, native Hawaiians, and locals, and it is much more. The various haole constructions of haole over the last two centuries all share in the effort to justify and naturalize haole presence in Hawai'i. At first, haole was about claiming and saving the islands, with explicit use of the ideologies of white supremacy and manifest destiny to justify its imperial desires. With that project largely completed with annexation, haole began to sing a very different tune. Rather than aggressively claiming white privilege, haole attempted to blend in, particularly by pretending to become native. Recently, haole has been bent on portraying itself as a victim, and I will discuss this in chapter 4.

Native Hawaiian and local constructions of haole remind us of the contestations inherent in colonial processes, as well as the relational nature of racialization. The interrelated counternarratives of haole highlight the legacies of colonization. While in certain instances they tend to fix haole, there have always been elements in both native and local constructions that recognize the dynamism, contingency, and interrelated nature of these racial productions. With this comes the awareness that one is never just haole, local, or native Hawaiian, and that the way one inhabits any one of those categories is always in process.

## CHAPTER 3

# "EH, HAOLE"

## Is "Haole" a Derogatory Word?

"Eh, haole." It is a phrase so common to Hawai'i that it must be spoken thousands of times an hour. Yet if an increasingly vocal group of haoles get their way, we will no longer be uttering the "H-word." In chapter 2 I explored the multiple constructions of haole generated over the years in haole, local, and native Hawaiian communities. An understanding of this variation, and the history of haole colonialism, is generally missing from the movement to ban "haole." Debates over "haole" as derogatory surface in popular media every few years, usually sparked by some incident of alleged name calling. Attempts to ban "haole" can be thought of as the flip side of haole attempts at positive self-constructions discussed in the last chapter (discoverer, savior, Hawaiian at heart, etc.). These constructions try to make space for those of us identified as haole in Hawai'i by providing escape hatches out of haole. Motivated primarily by a desire to belong, which includes an obscuring of white privilege, we want to at least be "Hawaiian at heart"; we certainly do not want to be haole.

The most omnipresent and disturbing construction of haole today is that of victim of alleged discrimination and prejudice, what on the continent might be referred to as "reverse racism." The notion of haole victimization is certainly not new, but it is now significantly bolstered by the Supreme Court's 2000 decision in *Rice v. Cayetano,* which called all Hawaiian entitlements into question as potentially illegal racial advantages. I explore the *Rice* case and other legal battles in the next chapter. Here I focus on the idea that the term "haole" is a racial slur and therefore part of haole victimization.

I begin with a look at the etymology (word origins and modifications over time) of the term and how we can understand that history today. I explore examples of the recurring debate about "haole" as pejo-rative, focusing on (1) a controversy at the University of Hawai'i involv-ing a haole student and Professor Haunani-Kay Trask; (2) the 1995 Hawai'i Civil Rights Commission ruling that "haole" is not deroga-tory; and (3) a 2004 uproar over a column by Jade Moon in which she declared "the H-word" neutral. These controversies illustrate the tenacity of the debate and highlight its shifting contours. In the sec-ond part of the chapter I analyze the two dominant racial discourses in the islands—racial harmony and racial conflict—to provide some con-text for understanding the debate over "haole." I demonstrate how the debate is caught in the binary between these two and suggest that an emerging discourse focused on racial production offers hope for break-ing us out of this cycle.

## Etymology and the Debate over "Haole"

An exploration of the etymology of "haole" reveals a bit more about Kanaka Maoli constructions of haole. The word "haole" was used in precontact days, although its exact meaning is uncertain (and would likely be nearly impossible to convey in translation to English). Its ear-liest use seems mostly to refer to things that were foreign or not from Hawai'i. The Pukui-Elbert Hawaiian dictionary gives its definition as "White person, American, Englishman, Caucasian; American, English; formerly, any foreigner; foreign, introduced, of foreign origin, as plants, pigs, chickens" (Pukui and Elbert 1986, 58).

It seems that the word's general evolution in meaning went from foreign, to white person, to its complex set of meanings today reflect-ing over two hundred years of colonization and its crossover from native Hawaiian to Hawai'i Creole English (HCE). It is popularly understood today in HCE to refer to white people and is also a marker of a certain set of attitudes and behaviors that are distinctly not local, reminding us that racial constructions always include more than skin color. Although some continue to hold on to the "foreigner" definition, I have yet to hear a recent South Asian immigrant or African American called "haole" as a descriptive label.

It is worth noting that I found a folk etymology of "haole" popping up everywhere in my research, even among well-respected scholars. It is frequently reported that "haole" originally meant "without breath." This meaning is derived from splitting the word, adding emphasis to the "a," and adding a glottal stop: "hā'ole," "hā" meaning "breath" and "'ole" meaning "without" or "lacking" (diacritical marks are critically important in Hawaiian, signifying different pronunciations that, in turn—given the oral tradition—constitute different meanings). One interpretation of "hā'ole" is that it referred to haoles' handshake greeting, which differed from the Kanaka Maoli rubbing of faces and sharing of breath. A slightly different version says the term indicated that haole were not to be greeted in this traditional way by Kanaka Maoli. Yet another interpretation says that haoles' pale skin indicated that they were not breathing.

Hawaiian language scholars, including Noenoe Silva, Pili Wilson, and Kanalu Young, doubt the "without breath" stories. Young says, "People who don't know the Hawaiian language assume you can divide a Hawaiian word pretty much anywhere you want. . . . It is untrue that you can slap these two together and determine that as [its] true meaning" (as quoted in Haire 2007). Pili Wilson says she thinks someone made this story up during her lifetime: "People like to make up little poems or stories about place names or words" (as quoted in Adams 1995). The fact that this interpretation persists, however, flags a continuing Kanaka Maoli desire to mark haole as outsiders, those to be regarded with a well-developed caution.

In 1990, an exchange in the University of Hawai'i Mānoa student newspaper, *Ka Leo,* between Professor Haunani-Kay Trask and undergraduate Joey Carter launched a huge controversy over the word (Carter 1990, *Ka Leo O Hawaii* Editors 1990).[1] The firestorm centered on an article in which Carter complained about being called "haole," and a letter from Trask responding. In the hurricane of letters, petitions, articles, forums, cartoons, and flyers that followed, the frame was shifted from a discussion of haole and Hawai'i's history of colonization to a debate over whether or not Trask was being racist in her response to Carter. Calling someone "haole" was likened to calling someone "nigger." Similarly, the experience of being a haole in Hawai'i was equated with being African American on the continent (*Ka Leo O Hawaii* Editors 1990). Trask's letter was said to constitute harassment, and many (led by faculty from the University of Hawai'i Philosophy Department) called for her removal from her position as director of the Center for Hawaiian Studies. Trask fought back and ultimately was not fired.

In 1995, a case before the state Civil Rights Commission made the news. A former haole employee sued her local Japanese employer, charging he used "haole" as a racial slur against her. Amidst the controversy,

the *Honolulu Advertiser* editorialized that "haole" could be "either inno-
cent or offensive, depending on its use" (Talking *Haole* 1995). The Civil
Rights Commission ultimately agreed, ruling against the employer
because he called the employee "fucking haole," but maintaining that
"haole" by itself was not a slur (a decision that resonates with Turnbull's parsing of the three different types of haole discussed in the previous chapter) (Matsunaga 1995). The public discussion remained on the
level of semantics without delving into the processes of colonization and
racialization from which haole originates.

Reporter Vicki Viotti followed up a month later with a feature
article in the *Honolulu Advertiser,* "Haole: Is It a Dirty Word?" (1995).
Viotti interviewed a number of people and investigated the etymology
of the word. The responses she got speak to the continuing contentious-
ness of the term: a few haoles, including University of Hawai'i ethnic
studies professor Noel Kent and "Haole boy" playwright Mark Pinkosh
tried to put a multicultural gloss on it; a local haole understood its
nuance; a local Asian student was ambivalent about it (or perhaps just
uninterested); most haoles were offended by it; and again, Hawaiian
studies professor Kanalu Young was the only one to attempt to contextualize it. If the article was successful at anything, it was reinforcement
of the divergent interpretations of the word, which suggests that perhaps Viotti's question was misguided.

Emboldened by the anti-Hawaiian lawsuits and a growing haole
population, attacks on the term have escalated in the last few years.
Letters to the editor sections of local newspapers frequently run letters
calling for banning the word, often attacking those who use it publi-
cally. Hawaiians and locals write back that the word is not derogatory
at face value; a few suggest one has to consider history and context, but
this is rarely given much attention. And back and forth it goes, stuck in
dualistic thinking that allows for only one of two answers, derogatory
or not.

In 2004 another controversy erupted when *MidWeek* columnist Jade
Moon published a piece titled "The H Word Is Harmless in Hawaii"
in response to e-mails she had received from readers (Moon 2004). The
first e-mail referred to the folk etymology of "haole": "Haole is a dero-
gative word, it literally means without 'ha' (without the breath of life,
without spirit). I am a Caucasian person and have lived in Hawaii many
years. When people ask me, are you Haole? I say no. I have spirit, in fact
I have more spirit than many Hawaiians. Should I call them Haole?"

Another, from a haole teacher, instructed Moon to not "use the word Haole in your writing or public speaking. You may have been taught that it is acceptable to do so, but its use is degrading and offensive."

Moon responded in her column by noting how "haole" is used as a normal part of daily parlance and that the haoles she talked to do not find it offensive. She cited Jonathan K. Osorio, professor of Hawaiian studies, reminding readers that the word originally meant "foreigner" and was not "invented to denigrate a people," unlike "nigger," which comes up as a frequent comparison. Moon wrote, "Every day in Hawaii you hear the word haole over and over. It is uttered by nonwhites and white people alike, as a description, nothing more. It is not used to denigrate, except by those who are themselves hateful" (Moon 2004).

The column set off a rash of responses. Moon's defense of the use of "haole" was called "bigoted," "offensive," and "antiquated." She was told she cannot know how haoles feel since she is not white and that "racism is not only a 'white' problem." The use of "haole" was said to demonstrate this (Tumblin 2004). Another reader suggested that by Moon's logic, she should feel okay being called "Media Geisha" (Stanley 2004). Yet another sarcastically thanked her for the information and continued, "Now when someone calls me a haole I will simply smile with the superior knowledge that the term is not the problem" (O'Connor 2004). Other readers defended Moon. "Haoles that are offended by the term 'haole' should get a reality check. . . . Are we not to use Hawaiian words in Hawaii any more?" (Banner 2004). Refreshingly, a haole student from the continent wrote, "Because I choose to make Hawaii my home, I'm haole whether I like it or not. But I accept Hawaii on Hawaii's terms that were established before I came here" (Duncan 2004).

Having followed this discussion for over two decades now, it is difficult not to get frustrated at its repetitive nature. It seems there will always be haoles who insist "haole" is derogatory (especially given the fact that new haoles arrive every day). In fact, their voice is getting louder and demanding even more attention, especially through the invocation of the law. Rather than accept their framing of the argument, I want to step back and look broadly at racial discourse in Hawai'i so that this controversy can be considered in that context.

## Two Discourses of Racial Politics in Hawai'i

Two discourses of racial politics in Hawai'i have emerged from the processes of colonization. The first is the well-worn discourse of racial harmony that represents Hawai'i as an idyllic social paradise where there is no racial conflict or inequality. Frequently contrasting the islands with the "racist mainland," this discourse circulates among many communities. Those living in Hawai'i are so accustomed to hearing about how the islands are a "melting pot" and how the "aloha spirit" abounds that we tend not to consider the amount of work it takes to keep this narrative alive.

There is also a competing discourse of racial conflict that contends haoles and nonlocal people of color are disrespected and discriminated against in Hawai'i. Clearly, the charge that "haole" is a racial slur falls into this box. As negative referents for each other, these discourses in many ways reinforce one another. I look at the discourses separately, then explore their interrelationship in naturalizing haole (i.e., making haole seem like a natural part of Hawai'i).

*Racial Harmony Discourse*

The discourse of racial harmony has been given decades of play by academics, politicians, writers, and the Hawai'i Visitors Bureau. Sociologist Romanzo Adams is credited as the first person to describe Hawai'i as a "racial melting pot" in 1926 (Okamura 1998, 267), and the metaphor has been so often used that it is now considered common knowledge. The harmony model constructs Hawai'i as exceptional in its lack of racial prejudice, its egalitarian relations, and its opportunities for nonwhite upward mobility (this narrative got a huge boost with the election of Hawai'i-born Barack Obama). While all of this may be true to some extent, not much attempt is made to square this model with Hawai'i's colonial history, including Kanaka Maoli dispossession and haole hegemony.

In fact, it is not a coincidence that in the 1920s–1930s, when the model was first developed, racial tensions were particularly high in the islands. Unions were organizing plantation workers in solidarity against haole bosses, the haole oligarchy was pushing back, trying to maintain their stranglehold on politics and economics, and the infamous Massie affair erupted into national headlines. The Massie affair was arguably one of the biggest events of the century in the islands, surpassed only by the bombing of Pearl Harbor and the declaration of statehood.

In 1931 haole Navy wife Thalia Massie alleged she was raped by a "gang of local thugs" wandering Waikiki. When the jury deadlocked, unable to convict based on her inconsistent story and shoddy evidence,

Massie's mother and husband took matters into their own hands. They kidnapped and murdered one of the five men on trial, a native Hawaiian named Joseph Kahahawai. In the subsequent trial, the murderers were found guilty, but the judge commuted their sentences to one hour in his office. These sensational events gripped the islands, inflamed racial fears and hatred on the continent, and nearly brought martial law down on the territory.[2]

All of this spurred those in power to look for ways to squelch the image (if not the reality) of Hawai'i as a cauldron of racial violence and conflict. Lori Pierce writes that part of the solution was found in the "'discourse of aloha,' a way of speaking and writing about Hawai'i that celebrates ethnic diversity in such a way as not to threaten Haole hegemony. The discourse of aloha was used on a daily basis to disavow racial tensions and to distract attention from the prevalence of institutional racism" (Pierce 2004, 128). Pierce demonstrates how public celebrations like May Day/Lei Day were conceived of as part of the aloha project. She notes that these efforts also fostered the racial harmony narrative by suppressing public discussion of racial conflict and inequality (Pierce 2004, 145).

Through the lens of the harmony model, then, Hawai'i is perceived as an amazing "racial laboratory" and a model for the nation and even the world. Building off this model, Lawrence Fuchs ends his canonical *Hawaii Pono* thus: "Hawaii illustrates the nation's revolutionary message of equality of opportunity for all, regardless of background, color or religion. This is the promise of Hawaii, a promise for the entire nation and, indeed, the world, that peoples of different races and creeds can live together, enriching each other, in harmony *and* democracy" (Fuchs 1961, 449). So compelling (and selling) was this idea of Hawai'i's exceptionalism that it quickly became integrated into local discourse, political speeches, novels, and tourist propaganda. In fact, its perpetuation became critical as a key argument for those who championed statehood and needed to reassure a race-anxious continent that the natives were *not* restless, but rather docile and happy. Three key factors are said to form the basis for Hawai'i's racial harmony: the welcoming nature of the host culture (the omnipresent "aloha spirit"), the lack of a racial majority, and the high rate of intermarriage. While all of these claims have some basis, this discourse exaggerates and manipulates them while ignoring complicating data.

Today's "prostitution"—to use Haunani-Kay Trask's metaphor

(Trask 1993, 184)—of the aloha spirit allows it to be used as a powerful, free-floating signifier opportunistically invoked in order to assure everyone that they are not just welcomed, but invited to make themselves at home in Hawai'i. This is not to deny the aloha spirit—aloha *is* a Kanaka Maoli value emphasizing affection, compassion, and kindness. Trask and others are pointing to its commercial and political appropriation by non-Hawaiians. Rona Tamiko Halualani puts this appropriation in the context of misrecognition and reinscription by the dominant culture.

> The notion that "Hawaiians are inherently generous" is a vested rereading and (mis)recognition of the philosophical concepts of *aloha 'āina* (love and respect for the land), *Aloha* (sharing, exchange in reciprocity), and *'ohana* (family, kinship, and interdependence). These are reinscribings that mimic a native being and stand as distortions tightly guaranteeing a one-way line of compassion and charity. (Halualani 2002, 23)

The misrecognition of the aloha spirit into this compulsory "one-way line of compassion and charity" from Hawaiians to everyone else is particularly galling because of all the communities in Hawai'i, Kanaka Maoli have the least materially to give.

The lack of a racial majority and the high level of interracial marriage in Hawai'i are certainly two of the elements that make the islands unique. The problem comes when the literature overemphasizes these things or simply assumes their direct relationship with a lack of racial conflict. Regarding population statistics, Jonathan Okamura writes, "The emphasis on demographic population rather than social status, especially in reference to the term 'majority,' also masks the monopoly for political and economic power wielded by haoles as an oligarchy of planters, merchants, and politicians during much of Hawai'i's history from the late nineteenth century to the middle of the present century" (Okamura 1998, 276). Colonial environments almost always involve rule by a powerful outsider minority, and Hawai'i is no exception.

Similarly, regarding intermarriage, Okamura and others have asked that we question the easy attribution of meaning overlaid on the numbers. Okamura notes that while we might assume a certain level of racial tolerance given these data, we cannot necessarily conclude this leads to equality or harmony (Okamura 1998, 269). Other scholars show that when you disaggregate the numbers, the two communities with the most power, haoles and Japanese, have much lower rates of intermarriage than others (Kirkpatrick 1987). Excitement about intermarriage is also often tied to a historic fetishizing of "mixed race" children as the "golden" generation of our future, revealing some troubling assumptions about marriage and procreation, not to mention a literal fulfillment of the white desire to "go native" by becoming the other through offspring. Additionally, we might question the heterosexism revealed by these studies, especially in light of the fact that divorce rates continue to soar and people are increasingly constructing kinship relationships outside of the institution of marriage.

Understanding this historical construction of the discourse of racial harmony is necessary to analyze the ways in which it is deployed today. One area for concern is the backhanded way it is being used to undermine Kanaka Maoli indigenous claims to the islands. For example, one letter to the *Honolulu Weekly* complains that "the word haole should be sent into the coffin" and ends by proclaiming, "No one owns these islands; they will be here long after mankind is gone. Let's all work together and make them the best places to live on this earth rather than squabble and use racial slurs" (Borzych 2007). Also from the *Weekly* we get this defensive posturing: "We are not guests. We live here. Hawai'i should be for those who love it, not just those born a certain race" (Lee 2003). From the *Honolulu Advertiser* comes this letter, which sounds remarkably like a travel brochure: "There is no other place in the world where you will find people of different ethnic backgrounds getting along with each other. I am Hawai'i. You can be Hawai'i. Come see Hawai'i. Then live Hawai'i" (Jeong 2006). Here, not only is Hawai'i for you, but you can actually become not just Hawaiian, but Hawai'i itself.

All three authors situate themselves as proponents of racial harmony through their assertions of "Let's all work together" and "Hawai'i should be for those who love it" and "There is no other place in the world" like it. These seem like reasonable statements until you drill into them and realize that they are being used to make native Hawaiian claims and entitlements seem unreasonable and unfair. They help fuel the backlash against Kanaka Maoli claims by positioning the authors as fair, reasonable, and caring about Hawai'i. This moral position is made possible by characterizing native Hawaiians as those who "squabble and use racial terms" and make exaggerated claims to the land unjustly based on their race. Indigeneity is directly challenged: "no one owns these islands," "we are not guests," and "I am Hawai'i. You can be Hawai'i."

Attacks on native Hawaiian entitlements are part of a backlash against the resurgence of the Hawaiian sovereignty movement that began in the 1970s. This backlash is partly fueled by the larger reactionary movement in the United States as evidenced by the direct relationship between those leading the charge in Hawai'i and the right-wing groups assaulting affirmative action and native entitlements on the continent (Kauanui 2002). I further address this backlash in chapter 4.

### Racial Conflict Discourse

The discourse of racial conflict and discrimination against nonlocals (most often meaning haoles, but also voiced by nonlocal people of color) has been less prevalent than the racial harmony discourse. Or perhaps it is just less public since it works against tourism. Yet in the current climate of legal attacks against Hawaiian entitlements, it is gaining strength. This discourse holds that Hawaiians and locals exclude, discriminate against, and even attack nonlocals simply because of their nonlocalness. At its most benign, nonlocals complain they are ignored or that locals/Hawaiians are rude to them. More serious are charges of discrimination in housing, state services, and employment. At the far end of the spectrum are claims of property damage, verbal abuse, and physical violence.

This narrative has gone through a number of transformations. During the early colonial and territorial periods it mostly took the form of a fear of "savage" anti-white violence—stories surrounding the Massie affair are prime examples. It surfaced again in the 1970s largely in response to Governor George Ariyoshi's administration and policies. During this period, local Japanese were moving into positions of power, determined to hold on to them. Many promoted the characterization of haoles and Filipinos as "nonlocals" who were overrunning Hawai'i and needed to be kept out. Efforts were made to put caps on immigration and create residency requirements for state employment and welfare (Haas 1992, 63–67). While not all of these policies were successful (some were instituted, only to be struck down by the courts), they contributed to a sentiment against nonlocals. This period of exclusion of Filipinos from the local demonstrates the shifting borders of who is and is not considered local.

The racial conflict discourse has continued to the present day, even though biased institutional policies and inflammatory official rhetoric largely ended in the late 1970s (Haas 1992, 67). Complaints of unfair treatment circulate in popular media and haole social circles, often raised by new arrivals. The perception of anti-haole prejudice seems widespread on the continent, and it could be that this creates a self-ful-filling prophecy for some.[3] Take this example from a letter to the editor: "I did not believe my husband's recruiting employer when he warned us of the prejudice against haoles. We felt we were a well-rounded, cul-turally sensitive family who had lived in several other countries outside the United States without difficulties. I believe him now, and want to move home" (Ballard and Ballard 2000). Again, we see how this writer claims a high moral position for her family by describing them as "well-rounded" and "culturally sensitive." They had been all around the world and not had "difficulties," so clearly the problem in Hawai'i was not with them, but rather with those they came in contact with.

I do not mean to suggest that nonlocals, including haoles, are never discriminated against. Clearly there are instances where they are. What I am interested in is exploring the ways these two stories about racial politics in Hawai'i get used in order to naturalize haole. In the har-mony discourse, haole is just one color in the islands' multicultural rainbow, belonging just as much as any other group. In the conflict narrative, nonlocals, especially haoles, *should* be able to belong but they are unfairly targeted for discrimination and abuse. So, following these logics, haoles either belong, or should be able to belong, just like anyone else in Hawai'i. To question that belonging by disrupting the melting pot or contextualizing the racial conflict that exists is to be racist.

Those who have been in the islands for some time and still com-plain about prejudice against haoles often invoke both the racial har-mony and conflict narratives. They use the harmony narrative not just to undermine indigeneity, but also to chastise locals. To use racial labels like "haole," this strain of the argument goes, is to be a racist like those unevolved people on the continent. We all know that in Hawai'i, we are beyond that. We are a multiracial, multicultural land where everyone has aloha for everyone else. The trope of racial harmony is used here to suggest that talking about race or using racialized labels is disharmoni-ous and antithetical to local culture, when in fact something closer to the opposite is the case. Whether or not Hawai'i is more or less "racist" than the continent is not the point. The point is that race works differ-ently in the islands than on the continent, including being an everyday part of conversations.

It is particularly ironic when haoles specifically lecture Hawaiians about "the aloha spirit," a tactic that has come into increasing use recently with attacks on Hawaiian entitlements. For example, a letter to the editor regarding the Kamehameha Schools admission policy states, "The fact that Kamehameha Schools is private does not exempt it or its affiliates from abiding by the 'Law of the Aloha Spirit'" (Case 2005). Adding insult to injury, this writer turns the culturally specific Kanaka Maoli concept and practice of aloha into "Law," grossly distorting it and then admonishing Hawaiians for not practicing it the way she thinks they should.

While this may seem incredible, unfortunately, this letter simply echoes the rhetoric of the lawyers leading the charge to end all programs and preferences for Hawaiians. In an online chat coordinated by the *Honolulu Advertiser,* H. William Burgess, one of the leading attorneys of this movement, was asked about his motivations. He responded, "I do it just because I don't like to see the aloha spirit turned into apartheid. Hawai'i's too special for that" (Burgess 2007b). Elaborating on this, Burgess' group, "Aloha for All," states on its Web site, "Hawaii's gift to the world is the Aloha embodied daily in the beautiful people of many races living here in relative harmony." The next move is easy to guess by now: "It is not in keeping with the spirit of Aloha for the government to give one racial group land or money or special privileges or preferences from which all other racial groups in Hawaii are excluded" (Burgess 2007a). Haoles claim a morally superior, colorblind position by painting Kanaka Maoli as a greedy racial minority playing the victim in order to obtain special privileges.

Thurston Twigg-Smith, in his book attacking sovereignty, takes the economic tack to champion the aloha spirit. He suggests that "revisionist" histories are riling up Hawaiians who "easily could lash out in a quick and violent manner if lands they erroneously believe are theirs are not turned over to them"(Twigg-Smith 1998, 2). Among other things, he asserts, this makes tourism vulnerable. "Success of tourism is tied to the Aloha Spirit, a blending of all races in a place of rare beauty. This peaceful and productive combination distinguishes Hawai'i from the world's other scenic spots. The feeling, the spirit, needs to be protected. . . . Divisive tactics could severely damage it" (Twigg-Smith 1998, 2). Significantly, Twigg-Smith's aloha spirit works in concert with the appropriation of Hawaiian culture toward capitalist ends—it is both "peaceful *and productive.*" Following haoles who have gone before him, Thurston Twigg-Smith knows what is best for Hawai'i. Hawaiians are too simple, too easily led astray to know how best to protect their cultural practice of aloha.

## Constructing a Different Story about Race in Hawai'i

The polarized relationship between the two stories about race in Hawai'i feeds on itself, making it hard to see that a fuller understanding may lie in reconsidering how we ask the question. If the question is not about whether or not "haole" is derogatory, what is it? How can we break out of the racist/not racist dyad? Is there a different way to understand racial politics in Hawai'i?

Some Hawai'i scholars have argued for a more historically based, political, and economic examination of racial politics in Hawai'i. This means looking at the processes of racial production and how they are tied to political, economic, and social power, rather than assuming race as an unproblematic concept. It means disrupting the entrenched discourse of racial harmony *without* overemphasizing or sensationalizing racial conflict. This is possible, but only through an understanding of colonization and racial production in the islands.

> Boundaries between groups are relatively fluid, and overt conflict is minimal. Hawaiian society lacks ethnically based group violence and is marked by a high level of interpersonal sharing and tolerance. . . . The myth of multicultural harmony, however, obscures enduring patterns of racism and exclusion, now directed particularly toward people of Hawaiian, Filipino, and Pacific Islander descent. The façade of harmonious multiculturalism conceals long-standing racial discrimination and persisting inequalities. (Merry and Brenneis 2003, 16)

Note that Sally Engle Merry and Donald Brenneis acknowledge "enduring patterns of racism and exclusion," but particularly against segments of the local, not haoles.

This analysis is borne out in other scholarship as well. John Kirkpatrick attributes the relative lack of manifest racial conflict in Hawai'i to some of the same factors as the racial harmonizers, but significantly also includes "haole domination" for the work it does to stamp out local and Hawaiian resistance (Kirkpatrick 1987, 301). Without downplaying haole power, Beth Bailey and David Farber attribute the latitude given Black soldiers during World War II to Hawai'i being more progressive on the issue of race than the continent—"the lines were less absolute, the barriers more permeable" (Bailey and Farber 1993, 819). Phyllis Turnbull and Kathy Ferguson remind us to attend to the intersected nature of all social relations in the islands.

> Central to the streams of order that converge and rebound on Hawai'i's present are particular organizations of sex, race, and class as triads of vectors of power: sex/gender, race/ethnicity, and class/property. . . . The terms of these energetic, interactive triangles chase and dodge around one another, powerfully enabling each other while sometimes getting in each other's way, confounding their dance steps. (Turnbull and Ferguson 1997, 99)

Scholars of local identity worry about the ways both the racial harmony and the conflict discourses tend to homogenize the local and disregard the indigeneity of native Hawaiians. While Kanaka Maoli may be considered part of the local today, their history is clearly longer and different from the immigration and plantation experiences that formed the local. John Rosa writes, "Local is a cultural identity, but it is also an inherently political identity that can be used by those who wish to gloss over and minimize the historical differences between Hawaiians and non-Hawaiians" (Rosa 2000, 101). Jeff Chang voices a similar concern.

> When Asian American scholars discussed the idea of the Local, they de-emphasized the tensions and conflicts inherent in its formation. They argued that this new panethnic identity intended to supplant oppressive, unequal relations with pluralistic, egalitarian relations. But even a radically plural conception of the Local tended to mask over large gaps in status and power between Asian and Pacific Islander ethnic groups. (Chang 1995, 25)

In arguing for a less rigid, more nuanced understanding of the local, Louise Kubo writes, "Communities do not travel or 'progress' in straight lines. Because they are inherently made up of multiple intersecting relationships, communities twist and turn, double back, and sometimes end up not very far from where they began" (Kubo 1997, 7). Kubo reminds us of what we know, especially living in Hawai'i: communities are dynamic and porous, not static and impenetrable. It is impossible to draw solid lines around local, native Hawaiian, or haole—they "confound each other's dance steps."

It is not often in the popular media that the discussion of race relations in the islands gets the kind of more complicated treatment demonstrated by the scholars above. Mostly we see self-congratulatory stories about our ethnic paradise or hand-wringing about incidents of racial violence that are treated episodically, fostering an amnesia that forecloses deeper thinking about the systemic causes of violence. Still, there are moments when the sun breaks through.

One example is an article that ran in 1999 in the *Star-Bulletin* titled "State's History Nurtures Ethnic Animosity: The Way People Treated Each Other through the Years Is Not Forgotten" (Kreifels 1999b). Reporter Susan Kreifels wrote, "Caucasians first wrested land and culture from native Hawaiians, oversaw Asian laborers sweating on sugar plantations, and went home to all-white neighborhoods." Kreifels talked to ethnic studies professor and native Hawaiian scholar Davianna McGregor, who reminds us that attitudes toward haoles "will be negatively colored until past injustices are atoned" (Kreifels' paraphrase). McGregor also notes that most haole newcomers are not used to being in a situation where whites are the minority. She cautions, "People come and don't expect to assimilate to Hawaii, they expect Hawaii to assimilate to America. That's unacceptable." Thinking that Hawai'i is for you is a key element of haoleness.

Columnist Vicki Viotti (author of the previously mentioned article "Haole: Is It a Dirty Word?") reflectively writes in a 2004 column about "realizing that there are issues of racial bias here I may not pick up because I'm, as we say, haole. Or, maybe I only recognize it when it's about my haole-ness" (Viotti 2004). As we have seen, it is no small thing to publicly recognize one's haoleness. And even rarer is the admission that being haole often has certain liabilities, including ignorance about certain racial dynamics. Again, part of what defines performative haoleness is a certain arrogance of ethnocentrism and certainty of knowledge.

A workplace column in the *Star-Bulletin* (an unlikely location for enlightened discussions of race) also suggested a local understanding of haole. Noting that "many people from the mainland United States find the word 'haole' to be offensive," this columnist advises that "the tone of voice used when 'haole' is spoken needs special attention. When the term is used with a pleasant tone of voice, the term can be descriptive rather than evaluative" (Brislin 2005). "Eh, haole, you seen my cell?" is altogether different from "Eh, haole, you can shut up an' let someone else speak or wat?" Brislin gives a similar example in the column:

> If people say, "The haole guy who was the first to speak at the union meeting" with a sneer in their voice, they are probably referring to a shared negative stereotype. These can include perceptions that mainland Anglos always have opinions about which they are extremely confident, speak in a very loud voice, and think they know how to run things after living in Hawaii for only a few months. (Brislin 2005)

As evidenced in this column, there is a tendency to want to argue that "haole" can be a "neutral" or purely descriptive term. It is not hard to see why that would be the case, against the tide of people arguing that it is derogatory and racist. The Hawai'i Civil Rights Commission, the *Honolulu Advertiser*'s editorial board, Jade Moon, the above-mentioned workplace columnist, and innumerable others have argued this way. Mostly I agree with this, but I also hear Davianna McGregor when she says that the term will carry negative connotations until there has been atonement for the injustices done. Without getting into a discussion of what atonement, reparations, or reconciliation might look like, I think McGregor is right. Even in the most benign usage— "Eh, haole, you seen my cell"—the term continues to carry some of the weight of its colonial history, even if we rarely think of it in that way. The compulsion to argue otherwise is evidence yet again of binary thinking—the fear that admitting anything other than complete neutrality for "haole" is somehow a concession that it is always already (and mainly) pejorative.

Sometimes this argument gets made from a Hawaiian-language perspective. For example, in an interview Hawaiian studies professor Kanalu Young says it is not derogatory "if you just use the term in an everyday sentence and you're speaking Hawaiian or English. . . . It has no innate or intrinsic derogatory meaning. Having said that, over the years there have been examples of white people, or haoles, behaving very badly here" (Haire 2007). The thing is, there is nothing "innate or intrinsic" about language, especially when there is more than one language involved. Languages are as fluid as the cultures in which they are embedded, and which they help produce. Tracing etymologies can help us understand words better, but etymologies are not the final determination of meaning, especially with crossover terms. Additionally, Young finds it necessary to recognize the history of haoles "behaving very badly here," even if he does not connect that to changes in the meaning of the word.

I do not speak Hawaiian, so I am in no position to talk about how the meaning of "haole" may have evolved in that language. However, the popular debate over the term is primarily about its usage in HCE, and to a much lesser extent its crossover into Standard English. It is one of the many Hawaiian-language words picked up and utilized in HCE, and as I argued previously, it is one of the most important and powerful political words to be brought over. Therefore, it seems that to understand its meaning today, we need to study it as it is used in that language.

In contemporary HCE, "haole" is a descriptor for white people in Hawai'i and for a certain set of attitudes and actions I have labeled performative haoleness. To varying degrees, it carries with it the history of colonialism, as it was forged through that history. Because of that, even when used purely descriptively, it is not a completely neutral term, nor should it be. It reminds us of the violences perpetuated against the land and people of Hawai'i, violences that are not simply contained in the past but that spill over into our present. And it is important that we be reminded, even if that is not comfortable or we do not know how to respond.

This circles us back to the idea of Kanaka Maoli and local counterdiscourses of haole discussed in the previous chapter. "White," "Caucasian," and "Anglo" do not do the same work "haole" does in pushing back against the dominant narratives that seek to smooth over colonization and racial inequality. The term "haole" is historically and spatially specific. One is not generically white, but haole, in Hawai'i. Most white people are not used to being racially marked, especially when that marking carries a reminder of injustices that made and maintain white privilege. Part of becoming less haole, or more local, is beginning to understand all of this. Davianna McGregor is right that "haole" names historical injustice that fortified colonial hierarchies and white supremacy. And Phyllis Turnbull is right that our choice as haoles is not whether or not we will be called "haole," but what kind of haole we choose to be.

## Conclusion

So at the end of the day, what does all of this say about how we should understand the term "haole"? First, it should be clear by now that we have to get beyond the debate over whether it is a "bad" word or not. That is a trap. Words do not exist outside of the discursive, temporal, social, and political contexts that give them meaning, and that they help to create. That is why I fleshed out the two dominant discourses of racial politics in the islands and showed how both can be used to make space for haole in Hawai'i. Once we begin to move beyond the simplistic notion that racial politics is either harmonious or not—that the islands are either racially tolerant or racist—we can begin to more fully understand haole as well.

I am hopeful that a new discourse of racial politics in Hawai'i is emerging that takes nuance, complexity, and contradiction into account. Rather than smoothing them over, this discourse not only contextualizes haole, but highlights tensions between representations of racial harmony and conflict within the local, as well as local complicity in native Hawaiian dispossession. It provides a historical framework for native Hawaiian debates over identification by race, nation, and indigeneity. It disrupts haole attempts to claim victim status by centering a critical analysis of colonization and exposing processes of racialization.

## CHAPTER 4

# "Locals Only" and "Got Koko?"

## *Is Haole Victimized?*

The phrase "locals only" has existed in the islands for decades. It was so widely used that it was chosen in 1981 to name a now successful clothing line that churns out "Locals Only" T-shirts, bumper stickers, and other merchandise. Since local identity goes far beyond simple residence in Hawai'i, the phrase helps shape that identity by announcing its boundaries. It says there are, or should be, places and practices only for locals. Given the increasing encroachment of nonlocal development and tourism, it is not hard to understand the sentiment behind such a claim, yet some haoles read it as anti-haole.

"Got koko?" is a more recent catch phrase—yet another play on the "got milk?" ad campaign. "Koko" means "blood" in Hawaiian, so the phrase is an assertion of native Hawaiian identity, although not an uncomplicated one given the imposition of blood quantum requirements on native people. Politically, I read the question as a challenge to those who claim place for themselves in Hawai'i, who may even claim to be Hawaiian, but who have no native ancestry. In some ways it might be a response to "locals only" in that it suggests, while you may be local, unless you have Hawaiian blood, you really do not belong in Hawai'i. It is seen by some haoles as militantly anti-haole.

I use these two phrases to frame this chapter in order to begin questioning the assumed direct relationship between them and alleged haole victimization. Many social movements, organized around building consciousness and political power in racialized communities, have been viewed as threatening to white people—think, for example, about white resistance to the Black Power movement and to Chicana/o organizing. Is it possible to understand the relationship between carving out space and identity for locals as more complex than simply anti-haole?

Is it possible to understand the assertion of indigenous ancestry as a statement of pride and deep connection to place existing prior to, and therefore in some ways outside of, relations with haole? Is it possible to understand both "locals only" and "got koko?" as assertions against colonialism (and toward decolonization), rather than reduce them to the ahistorical rhetoric of "reverse racism"?

The discourse of haole victimization is growing in the islands, emboldened by court decisions in favor of haole claims of reverse discrimination with respect to native Hawaiian programs and entitlements. As discussed in the previous chapter, the notion of haole victimization is closely tied to the narrative of racial conflict and has a long history. In that chapter we looked at the question of "haole" as a pejorative. I argued that instead of getting caught in a binary of arguing over whether Hawai'i's culture is fundamentally racist or not racist, the discussion should be turned to questions of racial formation, especially racialization (the processes through which people are raced) as an essential aspect of colonization. Haole worked to establish itself as the center or norm in the islands by constructing native Hawaiians and then locals as outside the norm, as racialized others, uncivilized, and un-American. Local and Hawaiian counternarratives of haole recognize and talk back to this history.

I begin this chapter with an examination of the charge that widespread physical assaults are part of the victimization of haoles. I look at hate crime data collected since 2002 but find it impossible to draw any overarching conclusions. There have not yet been any studies providing quantitative analysis to help us interpret the charge of widespread violence. Instead there are anecdotes and sporadic incidents that get talked about and occasionally reach the media, feeding a discourse of persecution and building a climate of fear. I give specific attention to pervasive narratives about anti-haole violence in public schools, in particular the oft-mentioned "kill haole day." I also analyze the 2007 Waikele beating of a haole military couple and the controversy it stirred over hate crimes. This incident hit a nerve in the general public where racial tensions have been escalating over the last decade.

I then look at the "reverse racism" claims made against native Hawaiian programs, entitlements, and preferences, giving particular attention to a number of lawsuits since 2000. The basic charge behind these cases is some laws, policies, and practices are victimizing haoles (and all non-Hawaiians) by giving Kanaka Maoli unfair advantages.

Since these arguments are founded in a colorblind ideology that insists we live in a postracial world with an equal racial playing field, I end with a consideration of socioeconomic data. These data literally flesh out the stark realities of the health and well-being of the native Hawaiian population relative to others in the islands. They require us to consider claims of haole victimization against the material consequences of processes of colonization that consolidated economic and political power for haoles primarily by dispossessing and subordinating native Hawaiians.

## Hate Crime and School Stories

In considering the question of whether haoles are victims, the obvious place to start is with incidents of violence. Hawai'i belatedly passed a hate crimes bill in 2001 and began collecting hate crime statistics, including data on attacks motivated by racial bias. Significantly, what legally counts as a hate crime in Hawai'i is different from the U.S. national norm. The FBI and most states base their statistics on police reports. Hawai'i, on the other hand, counts only those crimes actually prosecuted as hate crimes. The attorney general's office justifies this, saying it "eliminates false positives" (Dooley 2007), yet it appears to be eliminating a good deal more when you consider the numbers.

In 2002, the first year of data collection, only two hate crimes were prosecuted, one of which included "anti-white" elements. One hate crime per year was prosecuted in the next three years, all of them categorized as anti-white. In 2006 the prosecution spiked and six hate crime cases went to court; only one of them was anti-white (Perrone 2002–2005). Brian Levin, director of the Center for the Study of Hate and Extremism at California State University San Bernardino, called the low numbers reported by Hawai'i "absurd," adding that "some states dutifully collect data and others don't" (Dooley 2007). Given the size of O'ahu's population alone, it is difficult to believe there is not more hate crime. FBI statistics underscore these suspicions. States with comparable populations reported at least twice the number of hate crimes in 2006. Even New Mexico, which is also a "minority" majority state with a comparable population and the "land of enchantment" (according to their visitors bureau), reported twenty incidents (FBI 2006). There are political motivations for underreporting, as it clearly helps bolster the racial harmony narrative.

Despite the low numbers, one might be tempted to look at the ratio of four anti-white crimes out of eleven in the last five years and conclude that haoles are not disproportionately victimized (haoles are 40 percent of the population), but the data set is really too small, and its collection too riddled with questions, to draw any significant conclusions. Regardless of this lack of substantive data, there have always been stories about haoles getting beat up for being haole. It is impossible to know how many of these stories are based in actual incidents, and, taken out of context and proportion, they create a climate of fear and strengthen a sense of haole victimization.

When haoles talk about anti-haole violence, they often reference "kill haole day" in the public school system—a recurring event when haole kids were supposedly targeted for violence and humiliation. There are mixed opinions and only anecdotal evidence about how widespread the practice was and when it existed. In my research I found that the day was discussed by the state legislature in 1999 in a debate over passage of the hate crimes legislation. Significantly, while expressing concern, the representatives were unable to point to any concrete incidents (Gima 1999). Department of Education (DOE) spokesperson Greg Knudsen is quoted as saying, "Just about everyone in Hawaii is aware of the stories. But I've never seen any evidence that it actually existed" (Kreifels 1999b). Ironically, even without evidence, some legislators actually argued *against* a hate crimes bill because they feared the alleged practice of "kill haole day" would open the state to lawsuits if such a bill passed (Gima 1999). Perhaps they thought that with a hate crimes law, a flood of previously silent victims would come forward. So far, that has not happened.

Despite, or perhaps because of, the lack of documented incidents, the specter of "kill haole day" has taken on a life of its own. There are frequent references to it in local haole narratives, along with stories of schoolyard harassment. Charles Memminger, a columnist with the *Star-Bulletin*, has written on more than one occasion about being tied to a desk in an Aiea elementary school classroom. "We few haoles at Aiea didn't have to wait for kill haole day to be subjected to abuse. That could happen any day of the year. I have often related the time I was tied to a desk in class and the teacher walked out" (Memminger 2006).

"Kill haole day" also shows up in local literature as authors both draw on, and produce, the tropes of local culture. During and after the plantation era, public schools were a key site for the construction of local culture, especially as students resisted the Americanization forced upon them.[1] It seems likely that any instances of "kill haole day" violence would be more prevalent several decades ago. It also seems likely that haole boys were the primary targets and that they were disinclined to report because they were trying to protect their masculinity. Equally likely is that the threat of "kill haole day" was used as a bullying tactic. Without evidence, however, this is simply conjecture.

What about less spectacular forms of anti-haole harassment in the schools? Keeping in mind the history of public schools briefly discussed in chapter 1, the importance of schools in the construction of local identity, and reconsidering Davianna McGregor's caution that haoles should not expect Hawai'i to assimilate to America (Kreifels 1999b), we might reconsider the way we frame our questions. For example, to what extent is harassment fueled by resentment of historical haole domination and exercised against all haoles, and to what extent does it target those students who do not assimilate but continue to "act haole"? One key element here is language. Are haoles fluent in HCE, an important marker of localness, as likely to be targeted? Additionally, how do gender and class play into all of this?

This returns us to consideration of performative haoleness, which at its root may be largely attitudinal. Performative haoleness is founded in colonial attitudes of superiority and indifference to place and local cultures, attitudes that are certainly masculine in origin but espoused by women as well. As suggested previously, it manifests in behavioral excesses: being too loud, taking up too much space, demanding too much attention, and acting with disregard to local custom. The more one is able to appreciate and acculturate to local social norms and island cultures, the more one is able to mitigate one's haole quotient, and perhaps even earn the title of "local haole."

A 1978 study of a fifth-grade classroom in a rural elementary school, a time and place when and where resistance to haole dominance was high, supports this thinking about haole performance. Researcher Glen Grant writes, "The haoles in this study did not receive hostile behaviors from locals simply because they were haole, but because they performed specific behaviors and failed to negotiate specific contracts which would create the conditions for friendly interracial contacts" (Grant 1978, 595).

While I have argued elsewhere that Grant tends to gloss over racial tension in order to support the racial harmony narrative, his conclusion here is in line with other scholarship and my own anecdotal experience as a haole in a rural elementary school in the 1970s. I quickly learned to find ways to fit in or, more often, to not stick out so much. If acting haole means behavioral excess, it makes sense that not sticking out, or finding ways not to be noticed, is an important antidote. This is not to suggest that some of my schoolmates were not harassed simply because they were haole, but to indicate that the more local or invisible we were able to behave, the less likely we were to be targeted. The tactics of making oneself smaller and less assertive are clearly gendered female, suggesting fruitful avenues of research into the intersections of gender and haole.

Although there seem to be fewer references to "kill haole day" as a contemporary phenomenon, harassment of haole and African American students has made the news a handful of times in the last decade. A *Star-Bulletin* article in 1999 titled "Is Trouble Brewing?" reports on a handful of incidents of mostly verbal harassment in public schools (Kreifels 1999a). Haole students report being called "haole bitch," "stupid haole," and "haole bastard." Many students talk about a segregated school culture with haoles, African American (mostly military) kids, and various local groupings forming tight cliques. In 2005 anti-Black racism erupted at Radford High School, generating considerable media attention. Radford students and teachers responded by organizing a rally to demonstrate the "true" school spirit as one of tolerance and cultural mixing, relying heavily upon the discourse of racial harmony (Viotti 2005). This response is not uncommon. What *is* uncommon are any clear reports of the extent of anti-haole violence in the schools.

## Waikele Beating and Racial Tension

Since the advent of the modern tourist industry in Hawai'i, when incidents of racial violence against haole adults were reported, they tended to get momentary media and political attention with lots of finger pointing but little analysis. The political establishment would admonish locals and Hawaiians to "show more aloha," the unspoken threat being potential negative effects on tourism and, hence, jobs. Individual haoles would feel emboldened to make sweeping generalizations about their mistreatment and their lack of safety. The discussion rarely rose to a level of considering the legacies of colonialism, including haole racism and violence against locals (and when haole military personal are involved, the consequences of living in the most militarized "state" in the nation were ignored). While in no way condoning or diminishing the violence, I am suggesting that this type of treatment has not been productive because it fails to look at either the scope of the problem or its root causes. This superficial response worked along with the broader discourse of discrimination and racial conflict, enabling a two-dimensional story of haole victimization.

It is possible that increased racial tensions in the islands over the last decade are making it harder to simply dismiss incidents of violence. Whether or not the conversation will move to a more complex, historically grounded analysis remains to be seen. Breaking with past convention, controversy over a brawl in the parking lot of the Waikele Shopping Center in 2007 erupted into local news and garnered national coverage. It provides a window into thinking about increased racial tensions and a current case study regarding the question of haole victimization. At the heart of the issue was an argument over whether or not the incident should be prosecuted under Hawai'i's new hate crimes statute as anti-haole violence.

Different versions of the story are recounted, but the basic facts are now part of the criminal record. An argument broke out after a minor car accident in a shopping center parking lot on February 19, 2007. Gerald Pa'akaula, who is part Hawaiian, was sentenced to five years in prison for assaulting a haole military couple, Dawn and Andrew Dussell. Pa'akaula's sixteen-year-old son, who was also involved, was sentenced to a year at the Youth Correctional Facility. Apparently the Dussells hit the Pa'akaulas' car while pulling into a neighboring parking stall. Gerald Pa'akaula was getting ice cream for his family and, on his way back to the car, saw his wife and son engaged in an altercation with the Dussells. He became enraged and jumped into the fray. According to a *Star-Bulletin* article, Andrew Dussell was knocked unconscious, lost a front tooth, fractured an eye socket, and suffered a concussion. His wife's nose was broken. Pa'akaula's wife had a bloodied lip and his son suffered bruises and swelling to his face, arms, and back (Barayuga 2005).

The question of whether or not the incident qualified as a hate crime was raised because both Pa'akaula and his son called Andrew Dussell a "fucking haole" several times. Prosecutors decided against using the hate crimes charge, arguing instead that the incident was primarily motivated by road rage and not race. Hawai'i's hate crimes statute requires evidence that the victim was "intentionally selected" by the perpetrator "because of hostility toward the actual or perceived race, religion, disability, ethnicity, national origin, sexual orientation" of that person (Perrone 2002–2005). Even though the assault was not prosecuted as a hate crime, Circuit Judge Steven Alm raised the issue of race in his remarks at the time of sentencing. He warned that race relations in the islands are in a "fragile and delicate balance" and that this incident did not help the situation (Dooley 2005).

In the months between the February beating and the December sentencing, debate over the issue aired in local media despite the historical tendency to avoid giving these issues much coverage. In letters to the editor there were those who argued that "haole" is a Hawaiian word and not derogatory or hateful (as discussed in the previous chapter). There were those who said the attack was motivated by the accident or road rage, not racial hatred, and therefore did not qualify as a hate crime. There were those who said it was clearly a hate crime and the failure to prosecute it as such was a form of reverse racism. Just think what an outcry there would have been, these people argued, if the roles had been switched and it had been Hawaiians getting pummeled by haoles, especially military haoles. The *Star-Bulletin* editorial board weighed in, supporting the attorney general's office: "Prosecution of hate crimes is rare in Hawaii, not because of the state's racial, religious and sexual harmony, but because bigotry must be, beyond a reasonable doubt, the cause" (*Honolulu Star-Bulletin* Editorial Staff 2007).

Two University of Hawai'i professors represent the polarized positions on the incident. Jonathan Okamura in ethnic studies saw it as a hate crime because of the way the Pa'akaula father and son focused on Dussell's race. "Why did he focus on the fact that [the man] was haole? That wasn't the issue. The issue was damage to his car" (Pang 2007). For Okamura and many others, the repeated use of "fucking haole" made this a hate crime. He also pointed out that hate crimes have an intimidation factor and said, "I imagine haoles throughout Hawai'i, if they heard about the incident, are very concerned about the possibility of that happening to them" (Pang 2007).

On the other hand, professor and chair of Hawaiian studies Jonathan K. Osorio felt the races of the parties involved did not matter. "It worries me when people start calling something like this a hate crime because it starts to ramp up the public temperature over race in Hawai'i, and I don't think we need that" (Pang 2007). Those concerned about Hawai'i's image or the image of the native Hawaiian community often argue that using the hate crimes label simply makes matters worse, that the label somehow produces racial tension rather than simply describing an incident.

An article in *USA Today* about the incident titled "Racial Tensions Are Simmering in Hawaii's Melting Pot" is exactly the type of national publicity many in Hawai'i fear. The article opens by questioning the racial harmony narrative: "A violent road-rage altercation between Native Hawaiians and a white couple near Pearl Harbor two weeks ago is provoking questions about whether Hawaii's harmonious 'aloha' spirit is real or just a greeting for tourists" (Kasindorf 2007). The article also mentions a 2005 attack on haole campers at a beach on the Big Island (this was the one hate crime reported in 2005). University of Hawai'i law professor Jon Van Dyke notes that racial conflict does not often get much public airing in the islands because "it is like news about shark attacks. People are afraid they will lose customers" (Kasindorf 2007). Jon Matsuoka, dean of the University of Hawai'i School of Social Work, explains the reality obscured by the harmony narrative: "There is a notion that we have this kind of rainbow society and we all get along really swell. The reality is that there are racial tensions. They are deep-seated and historical, and that history didn't abruptly stop" (Kasindorf 2007).

The third paragraph of the *USA Today* article notes that this incident came at a time when the courts were "being asked to tackle another inflammatory racial issue . . . special benefits for Native Hawaiians, ranging from preference at an elite private school to free houses on government land." Besides overstating entitlements (very few Hawaiians actually get "free houses," for example), this statement accepts the conflation of Kanaka Maoli indigeneity with race (a dangerous slippage supported by the *Rice* decision and discussed in the next section). The next sentence describes entitlements as "perks." Later in the piece, John Goemans, lead attorney in lawsuits attacking entitlements, talked about how he moved to Beverly Hills out of fear of retaliation. "Well, 15,000 people marching—and I'm the guy they're looking for—is alarming." Here the massive peaceful demonstrations in support of Kamehameha Schools are represented as some sort of bloodthirsty mob.

In a more reasoned way, Dean Matsuoka supports the possibility of a connection between the backlash against native Hawaiian entitlements and the Waikele beating. He says what happened in Waikele could be "a random, isolated act, but on the other hand there have been all these encroachments on Hawaiian entitlements. I've thought for a long time that there would be growing anger and frustration on the part of the

Hawaiian populace" (Kasindorf 2007). This statement, combined with his earlier one about racial tensions in Hawai'i being "deep-seated and historical" helps to tone down some of the more inflammatory elements of the *USA Today* article by suggesting a larger context.

Useful here is the concept of structural violence, first articulated by peace studies researcher Johan Galtung to describe violence that is not direct but nonetheless harmful. Structural violence is so ingrained within social and political institutions that it is difficult to discern (Galtung 1969). Galtung's description of one aspect of the relationship between direct and structural violence provides a basis for thinking about anti-haole violence.

> Both direct and structural violence create needs-deficits. When this happens suddenly we can talk of *trauma*. When it happens to a group, a collectivity, we have the collective trauma that can sediment into the collective subconscious and become raw material for major historical processes and events. The underlying assumption is simple: "violence breeds violence." Violence is needs-deprivation; needs-deprivation is *serious;* one reaction is direct violence. (Galtung 1990, 295)

Tying this to Matsuoka's comments, direct violence is one outcome of "growing anger and frustration on the part of the Hawaiian populace" based on "deep-seated and historical" structural violence. Postcolonial scholars provide excellent analysis of the "trauma" of colonization experienced by the colonized, even if they do not call it that. Locally, Jonathan K. Osorio's book *Dismembering Lāhui* is in many ways all about the trauma inflicted on Kanaka Maoli through colonial processes that involved both direct and structural violence (Osorio 2002). I am suggesting that we keep this concept of structural violence in mind as we consider how to think about incidents like the Waikele beating and narratives of anti-haole violence. In a later section on socioeconomic data, the consequences of institutionalized "needs-deprivation" of Kanaka Maoli will become apparent.

## Hawaiian Entitlements, Preferences, and Programs Attacked

In chapter 1 I outlined some of the history of haole colonization that needs to be considered if we are to understand the current racial climate in the islands and the reasons behind programs and policies benefiting native Hawaiians. In this next section, I look at the charge that Hawaiian entitlements, preferences, and programs are simply unfair racial advantages and therefore part of the victimization of haoles. The recent onslaught of attacks against entitlements began with a lawsuit brought by Harold "Freddy" Rice, a fifth-generation haole of missionary descent, against the state of Hawai'i.

### Rice v. Cayetano

To understand the *Rice* case, one must first understand some background information regarding native Hawaiian legal status. Kanaka Maoli have a "special relationship" with the state of Hawai'i and the federal government based on the overthrow of the monarchy and the seizure of lands belonging to the Kingdom of Hawai'i. That special relationship is codified in numerable government documents, including the 1898 Annexation Resolution, 1900 Hawaiian Organic Act, 1921 Hawaiian Homes Commission Act (HHCA), 1959 Statehood Act, 1993 Apology Bill, and hundreds of federal laws addressing Native American, Alaska Native, and native Hawaiian affairs.

Most of the crown and government lands taken at the time of the overthrow (1.8 million acres, or approximately 43 percent of all land in Hawai'i) are now held in a Public Land Trust by the state.[2] Significant exceptions include Hawaiian Homelands and lands taken for federal or state use. Since 1921 the Department of Hawaiian Homelands has administered 200,000 acres of crown and government lands (commonly referred to as "ceded lands," although scholars and activists point out that the lands were never officially ceded to any government). The land given to the Department of Hawaiian Homelands is some of the worst land in the islands. Even more "ceded lands" (in this instance, some of the best land in the islands) are under the control of state and federal governments, including at least half of the 236,303 acres used for military facilities and training (Kajihiro 2007, 2–3).[3]

Even with these exceptions, the Public Land Trust still encompasses an enormous amount of property and generates millions of dollars annually in revenue. Since 1980 20 percent of the proprietary revenues (i.e., rent) generated from the Public Land Trust have been mandated to go into programs benefiting Kanaka Maoli (although that has not happened and lawsuits have ensued). These programs are administered by a state of Hawai'i entity, the Office of Hawaiian Affairs (OHA), which was voted into existence in the 1978 state constitutional convention.

Since OHA was set up to run programs for native Hawaiians, OHA trustees were voted for by native Hawaiians.

Harold Rice filed his lawsuit in 1996. Rice charged that OHA's Hawaiians-only voting restriction for trustees constituted unlawful racial discrimination. Four years later, in *Harold F. Rice v. Benjamin J. Cayetano*, 528 US 495 (2000), the U.S. Supreme Court agreed with Rice. In a 7–2 decision the Court held that the state violated the Fifteenth Amendment's ban on voting restrictions based on race. The majority opinion was written by Justice Anthony Kennedy, with Justices John Paul Stevens and Ruth Bader Ginsberg dissenting. I have argued elsewhere that the Court was able to come up with this ruling by reading Kanaka Maoli indigeneity as race, adhering to a colorblind ideology, and glossing the history of the U.S. colonization of Hawai'i.[4]

The impact of this decision has been tremendous because of the precedent it sets. It has spawned a flurry of other suits attacking native programs, entitlements, and preferences wherever they are found, including targeting OHA directly, the Department of Hawaiian Homelands, and the Kamehameha Schools admission policy of giving preference to Hawaiian students. The *Rice* decision has caused great concern for Kanaka Maoli who rely on government programs to make ends meet and support efforts toward cultural renewal. Into this charged atmosphere in 2000, U.S. Senator Daniel Akaka introduced his Native Hawaiian Government Reorganization Act, popularly known as the Akaka bill.

The Akaka bill has undergone multiple revisions to try to make it palatable to Congress, each one weakening it significantly. It has been introduced by the senator every year since 2000, except 2002, but has repeatedly stalled in committee. It purports to shore up government funding for Hawaiian programs by establishing some limited federal recognition of a vaguely defined Hawaiian "sovereign entity." Those who wholeheartedly support it, including OHA, tout it as granting the sovereignty Kanaka Maoli have been fighting for—or at least the closest approximation that can be reasonably expected.

Those sovereignty activists who stand adamantly opposed to the bill argue that it is just "another form of genocide" because it forces Hawaiians into an extremely compromised relationship with the U.S. government, similar to that of many Native American nations. Not surprisingly, those leading attacks on Hawaiian entitlements are also opposed to the bill, but because they see it as another example of racial preference. Their attacks are successful insofar as they are able to rehabilitate and retool the discourse of racial conflict and haole victimization using reverse racism rhetoric from the continent, but often putting it into a paternalistic neocolonial context. In this spin, haoles still know what is best for Hawaiians and Hawai'i. Harold Rice's own perspective is a case in point.

Keep in mind that Rice is a fifth-generation haole of missionary descent, a Big Island rancher, and someone familiar with local culture and Hawai'i's history. In an interview statement that parodies itself, Rice commented, "I wish the best for the Hawaiians. If anything, I'm pro-Hawaiian. . . . Most of my friends are Hawaiian" (Rice as interviewed in Sodetani 2003). He believes that through his lawsuit he is playing a positive role in history. "It was good for Hawaiians, and certainly good for the state. Got everybody thinking. Hawaiians took advantage of being able to play the part of victim and get entitlements based on race. They stepped over the line. The Rice decision made everyone step back" (Rice as interviewed in Sodetani 2003). In other words, regardless of history, Hawaiians ought to be treated like everyone else and ought to act like everyone else. The palpable, documented material and psychological impacts of colonization are to be ignored. Any attempt to address these legacies simply casts Hawaiians as "playing the part of victim."

In Rice's story, Hawaiians are *playing* victims, but are not in fact *true* victims (while Rice does not come out directly and say haoles are victimized by Hawaiians, he and his case lay the groundwork for that move). Following colorblind logic, Rice believes Hawaiians should not get special entitlements or receive "free handouts." In fact, he believes Hawaiians have the advantage in the islands. "Hawaiians are just as capable as anybody of doing well in today's world. They have the intelligence and ability and the advantage of this being their home, so they don't need the help" (Rice as interviewed in Sodetani 2003). According to Rice, Hawaiians have not been disadvantaged by colonialism. In a bitterly ironic twist, he contends that Hawaiians have the advantage because they are at "home"—a home his ancestors and other haoles have controlled for over a century. And then, in an essentializing gesture that reinforces the stereotype of the simple, carefree native, he stated, "Frankly, I've never run into a Hawaiian who wasn't smarter and more capable than me. I sort of kid that's why us haoles have to push and work so hard—we don't have the talent. I mean, if I could play music and sing like these Hawaiians, I wouldn't have to be so pushy, I'd be more happy, content" (Rice as interviewed in Sodetani 2003).

Not surprisingly, this notion of Hawaiians as "smarter and more capable" than haoles is not echoed by other haoles. It is evidence of Rice's own contradicted positioning, wanting to be friends with Hawaiians while at the same time laying the groundwork for the potential evisceration of Hawaiian programs. What does get picked up and amplified from Rice is the idea that haoles suffer because of unfair advantages given Hawaiians. Subsequent lawsuits have been spun in public discourse not only by mobilizing the Fourteenth and Fifteenth civil rights amendments' protections against racial discrimination, but also by cleverly twisting the racial harmony narrative and Hawaiian cultural practices into service.

*Kamehameha Schools Lawsuits*

Kamehameha Schools is a multicampus, private institution with an endowment of $6.8 million serving between five thousand and six thousand preschool to twelfth grade students in Hawai'i, making it the largest institution of its kind in the United States. It was founded in 1887 as part of the Bishop Estate, an enormous land trust established from the will of Princess Bernice Pauahi Bishop, the last direct descendent of King Kamehameha I. Princess Pauahi Bishop was very concerned about the suffering of her people and believed education was one of the keys to a better future. She instructed that Kamehameha Schools be established to provide "a good education" to boys and girls, giving preference to "Hawaiians of pure or part aboriginal blood" (Bishop 2008).

In the first case, the mother of a seventh-grade haole boy was able to get her son admitted by claiming he was native Hawaiian because she was hānai (a traditional Hawaiian practice similar to adoption) by a Hawaiian stepfather. This mother, Kalena Santos, argued she was Hawaiian through the cultural practice of hānai, and therefore her son, Brayden Mohica-Cummings, was also Hawaiian. When the school found out that Mohica-Cummings had no Hawaiian ancestry, it tried to rescind its enrollment decision, but Santos fought back and sued. In the December 2003 settlement, Kamehameha Schools agreed to allow Mohica-Cummings to remain enrolled in exchange for his mother dropping the suit.

The question of Mohica-Cummings' Hawaiianess, given the hānai status of his mother, led to all sorts of discussion and debate. Significantly for the study of haole, it opened up space for some haoles to admonish Hawaiians for not following their own culture. This statement by

Robert Rees is a prime example: "Kamehameha Schools—Hawai'i's pre-eminent guardian of Hawaiian culture and customs—rejected the great Hawaiian tradition of hānai in the name of preserving racial preferences" (Rees 2003). Kamehameha Schools fought back, vigorously maintaining that their preference for Hawaiian students was based on ancestry or genealogy and not race, yet this argument had been defeated in *Rice.* School officials and trustees were compared to George Wallace and other white supremacists barring the doors to the admission of Black students on the continent (Antone and Staff 2003). And so a haole boy was able to invoke the legacy of the civil rights movement, framing Hawaiians as unjust bigots.

Marcus Daniel, an associate professor of history at the University of Hawai'i, addressed this in commentary running on the same page of the *Honolulu Advertiser* with Rees.

> Whatever the faults of Kamehameha Schools (elitism for start-ers), it wasn't created to deprive white people of educational opportunity; it was created to provide opportunity for Native Hawaiians who had been deprived of educational opportunities by whites! Only to the willfully ignorant could such differences mean nothing. But in the resentful racial imagination of many American whites, the world is turned upside-down and whites become the "victims" of racial injustice. (Daniel 2003)

Here Daniel asks us to question the "upside-down" logic that assumes preferences or programs for Kanaka Maoli necessarily mean disadvantages for nonnatives, that attempts to provide opportunities for natives somehow necessarily deprive nonnatives. Other scholars and groups ask that we consider the very different histories behind the civil rights movement for African Americans and efforts by indigenous Hawaiians to reclaim their culture and nation. For example, the Web site SupportKamehameha.org states, "There is a critical difference between an affirmative action or diversity program and the efforts of a private institution to help an indigenous group almost wiped out by Western influence" (SupportKamehameha.org). Kanaka Maoli continually strug-gle to bring attention to the specificity of their colonial history.

It is worth noting that this lawsuit, bent on establishing white victimhood, was supported and funded by many of the same powerful haoles behind the *Rice* lawsuit. John Goemans, who convinced Harold

Rice to play the role of plaintiff in the first place, served again as lead attorney. To defeat Kamehameha Schools, Goemans pulled in financial backing from three powerful, rich haoles. These included James Growney, heir to the Campbell Estate, Thurston Twigg-Smith, former owner of the *Honolulu Advertiser* (and crusader against Hawaiian rights and sovereignty), and Scott Wallace, former owner of Wallace Theaters (Daysog 2003). As descendents of the haole oligarchy, Growney and Twigg-Smith's fortunes were built directly through the dispossession of the Kanaka Maoli and the industrial development of Hawai'i.

The second lawsuit against Kamehameha Schools for the admission of a haole boy—this time unnamed (*John Doe v. Kamehameha Schools*)—was also filed by Goemans in 2003 and was allegedly settled to the tune of $7 million in May 2007, according to Goemans' account. The suit moved between state court and the Ninth Circuit Court of Appeals for four years before lawyers for John Doe appealed an unfavorable (to them) circuit court decision to the U.S. Supreme Court. It is important to note that Kamehameha Schools and Hawaiian organizations organized vigorous public protest against both of these lawsuits. One march included more than ten thousand people, many wearing red shirts with the saying "Kū I Ka Pono"—Justice for Hawaiians.

In May 2007, before the Supreme Court could announce whether it would hear the case and in order to protect themselves from a possible precedent-setting negative outcome similar to *Rice,* Kamehameha Schools settled confidentially. In February 2008, Goemans leaked to the media that the settlement topped $7 million. This provoked an outcry against Kamehameha Schools from many native Hawaiians concerned that such a huge settlement could act as an invitation for more lawsuits (Dooley 2008).

Hawai'i attorney David Rosen promised just that the day after the settlement was announced. He used the media and e-mail to solicit plaintiffs (a move of questionable legality now under scrutiny by the Hawai'i State Bar Association) (Staff 2007) for yet another attack on the Kamehameha Schools admission policy. In launching this new attack Rosen said he thinks the "highest court in the land" should rule on the question and was disappointed that the John Doe suit settled. He said he is not motivated by money and will take only $1 in fees if the Kamehameha Schools lawyers do the same. He wrote, "Like many others in Hawai'i, I believe that consideration of an individual's national origin or race is immaterial for any reason other than human interest. . . . We cannot return to the past or undo it." In his e-mail solicitation Rosen promised "the identity of all of the plaintiffs will be kept extremely confidential" and "there will be absolutely no cost to the Plaintiffs" (KITV 2007). He also claimed to be motivated by the good of the children, not wanting his own "growing up as second-class citizens in their own home" (Rosen 2007). Thus in a few short sentences Rosen vanishes indigenous difference, sweeps centuries of colonial violence under the rug, and claims victimhood for his haole children.

Rosen filed his new suit, along with Eric Grant, on behalf of four anonymous students in August 2008. Remarkably, the attorneys proudly admit the suit is "essentially identical" to the original John Doe suit, the only difference being this time there are four Does and they will not settle. Eric Grant stated, "The purpose of today's action is to obtain a definitive ruling from the Supreme Court that the [Kamehameha Schools] trustees' racially exclusionary policy violates our nation's civil rights law." Rosen and Grant not only describe the plaintiffs as "representative of Hawai'i," but go even further to claim that "they are Hawaiian in every sense save the merely genetic" (Dooley and Pang 2008). This statement is clearly meant to undercut indigenous claims and highlights the anti-Hawaiian sentiment behind the case.

The attorneys drove home the now familiar claim that Hawaiians are turning Hawai'i into a place rife with racial strife and discrimination. "Our clients believe, and we agree with them, that such a ruling will have a significant impact in reversing unfortunate trends toward discrimination and even segregation in Hawaii" (*Honolulu Star-Bulletin* Staff & Associated Press 2008). Kamehameha Schools trustees countered: "It is deeply disturbing to see a Civil Rights law enacted to protect an oppressed population used to undermine Pauahi's desire to restore the vitality and health of her people, who were dispossessed in their own homeland" (Kamehameha Schools Board of Trustees 2008). Some alumni say they are happy to see the suit because it will settle the question once and for all (Dooley and Pang 2008). The trustees are showing a strong front, referencing the favorable Ninth Circuit Court decision, but as a Supreme Court case, *Rice* casts a much bigger shadow, and that clearly has them and the community nervous.

On another front, attorney H. William Burgess (whose rhetoric we examined in chapter 3) continues to hammer away at Hawaiian programs that receive state monies. Burgess organized the *Arakaki v. Lingle* lawsuit in which sixteen plantiffs sought to abolish OHA and the Department of Hawaiian Homelands. In April 2007 a district court judge dismissed the case because she found that the plaintiffs, suing simply as state residents, had no standing (Ferrar 2007). Burgess was undaunted and reorganized some of the same plaintiffs into another attack, this time on the new native Hawaiian registry, Kau Inoa. In July 2007 he requested that his five non-Hawaiian clients be added to the Kau Inoa register. His request was denied and OHA is bracing for another lawsuit. Clyde Nāmauʻo, OHA administrator, explained that the register is "for Hawaiians to come together and decide what their nation will look like. After forming a nation, they may choose to include non-Hawaiians the way other native nations have" (OHA Public Information Office 2007).

This section has provided a brief sketch of some of the recent lawsuits attacking programs, preferences, and entitlements granted to Kanaka Maoli. Beginning with Rice's successful suit against OHA in 2000, a group of primarily haole attorneys has honed a legal strategy that frames Hawaiian entitlements as forms of unlawful racial discrimination that disadvantage non-Hawaiians, particularly haoles. In popular parlance, Hawaiians are increasingly cast as unfairly taking advantage of the state, and all other Hawaiʻi residents, by playing the part of victims and demanding special treatment. In an ironic twist, Hawaiian programs and entitlements are said to go against the "aloha spirit" because they are "divisive" and unfair to non-Hawaiians.

## Socioeconomic Data

So far I have discussed how the notion of haole victimization rests primarily on claims of both physical violence and unjust racial discrimination. I now turn our attention to some demographic and socioeconomic data regarding different populations in Hawaiʻi, in particular comparing Kanaka Maoli with haoles. Keeping in mind that we are talking about racial constructions, not "natural" categories, it is telling that in study after study native Hawaiians consistently show up at the bottom of socioeconomic indicators. It is important to remember that all aspects of general health and achievement are interrelated. How well a child does in school is related to that child's physical health, which is related to his or her family's income level and assets, which is related to property ownership, and so forth.

Since Kamehameha Schools has been in the crosshairs, I start by looking at data on educational performance, the most extensive of which regarding native Hawaiian students is collected by that very institution. Of the estimated 70,000 school-aged Kanaka Maoli children in the state, Kamehameha Schools' total enrollment is only 4,856, or 7 percent (*John Doe v. Kamehameha Schools/Bernice Pauahi Bishop Estate,* 04-15044 U.S. Ninth Circuit Court of Appeals, 2006, 19058). A full 87 percent are enrolled in public schools, making 26 to 32 percent of all public school children native Hawaiian (Kanaʻiapuni, Malone, and Ishibashi 2005, 179, 182). Comparatively, only 13.6 percent of public school students are "Caucasian"—the label used in empirical data collection (State of Hawaiʻi Department of Business 2006). Part of this is explained by the historical pattern of haole flight to the many private schools in Hawaiʻi.

Not only does the general state of public education in Hawaiʻi today have a huge impact on Kanaka Maoli students, but its historical hostility toward Hawaiian culture has resulted in incalculable harm. Education has always been a primary force in colonizing a population, as discussed in chapter 1, and since annexation Hawaiʻi's public education has had Americanization as one of its primary goals (Tamura 1993). (Anecdotally, in my second-grade class at Kōloa Elementary, we began every day saying the Pledge of Allegiance and singing three to five patriotic songs. I remember belting out "America the Beautiful," whose lyrics probably meant little to my local classmates, and which excluded Hawaiʻi anyway as outside the parameters of "sea to shining sea.") State Department of Education (DOE) reliance on Western standardized tests, curricula, and content—not to mention the banning of Hawaiian language in the schools—have all worked against Kanaka Maoli students.[5]

Since the 1980s the federal government has gathered educational data on Kanaka Maoli students that show them falling far below average in performance and disproportionately represented in negative social, physical, and cognitive scales. Congressional findings of 2006 (based on data from a Kamahemeha Schools 1993 assessment) in Title 20 of the U.S. Code (also cited by Ninth Circuit Court Judge Graber in her opinion in *Doe v. Kamehameha Schools*) are illustrative, and I quote them here at length.

(A) educational risk factors continue to start even before birth for many Native Hawaiian children. . . .
(B) Native Hawaiian students continue to begin their school experience lagging behind other students in terms of readiness factors such as vocabulary test scores;

(C) Native Hawaiian students continue to score below national norms on standardized education achievement tests at all grade levels;

(D) both public and private schools continue to show a pattern of lower percentages of Native Hawaiian students in the uppermost achievement levels and in gifted and talented programs;

(E) Native Hawaiian students continue to be overrepresented among students qualifying for special education programs provided to students with learning disabilities, mild mental retardation, emotional impairment, and other such disabilities;

(F) Native Hawaiians continue to be underrepresented in institutions of higher education and among adults who have completed four or more years of college;

(G) Native Hawaiians continue to be disproportionately represented in many negative social and physical statistics indicative of special educational needs, as demonstrated by the fact that—

   (i) Native Hawaiian students are more likely to be retained in grade level and to be excessively absent in secondary school;

   (ii) Native Hawaiian students have the highest rates of drug and alcohol use in the State of Hawaii; and

   (iii) Native Hawaiian children continue to be disproportionately victimized by child abuse and neglect. (*Native Hawaiian Education,* U.S. Code, vol. 20, secs. 7512 [2006]).

An extensive 2005 report by Kamehameha Schools (available online) contains distressingly similar findings and offers analysis regarding how to think about and remedy these conditions (Kanaʻiapuni, Malone, and Ishibashi 2005).

The failure of public schools with regard to Kanaka Maoli students is one of the reasons given for the importance of Kamehameha Schools. In her opinion in *Doe v. Kamehameha Schools,* Judge Graber states,

In view of those facts and congressional findings, it is clear that a manifest imbalance exists in the K–12 educational arena in the state of Hawaii, with Native Hawaiians falling at the bottom of the spectrum in almost all areas of educational progress and success. Furthermore, it is precisely this manifest imbalance that the Kamehameha Schools' admissions policy seeks to address.

The goal is to bring Native Hawaiian students into educational parity with other ethnic groups in Hawaii. (*John Doe v. Kamehameha Schools/Bernice Pauahi Bishop Estate*, 19078–19079)

Educational inequality trickles up as well. In fall 2004, 7.9 percent of University of Hawai'i at Mānoa students fell under the category Hawaiian or part Hawaiian. When looking at University of Hawai'i community colleges, the percentage more than doubles for native Hawaiians (17.2) and plummets for haoles (16.1 in community colleges vs. 26.1 at Mānoa). Even more telling are faculty numbers. In fall 2003, 4.1 percent of faculty at Mānoa were Hawaiian and 61.9 percent were Caucasian (keep in mind that Kanaka Maoli are about 20 percent of the state's population and haoles are 40 percent when comparing "race alone or in combination" data from the 2000 Census) (Young 2006).

Health statistics for native Hawaiians are perhaps even more shocking. The *Native Hawaiian Data Book* is a good source for this information, as is the *Native Hawaiian Health Care Improvement Reauthorization Act* (January 30, 2007, version currently S. 429 in the 110th Congress) that Senator Daniel Inouye keeps introducing in Congress to no avail. This bill contains pages of findings regarding the "unmet needs and health disparities" plaguing Kanaka Maoli. They include a general cancer rate of 218.3 per 100,000, a rate 50 percent higher than the general population of the state, and a breast cancer rate 33 percent higher than the rate for Caucasian women. Asthma is a huge problem for Kanaka Maoli, with 12.8 percent of adults reporting asthma, a figure 71 percent greater than that of the total population. The mortality rate for heart disease is 86 percent higher than that of the total population. Hawaiians have the lowest life expectancy of all population groups in the state, averaging five to ten years fewer. Native Hawaiians have the highest infant mortality rate in the nation after African Americans, a rate 151 percent higher than that of Caucasian babies born in Hawai'i. The obesity rate for native Hawaiians is between 100 and 145 percent higher than the total population depending on how it is calculated. Native Hawaiians have the highest rate of smoking at 27.9 percent versus the state average of 17 percent. The prevalence of binge drinking is highest for native Hawaiians, and the prevalence of heavy drinking is 33 percent higher than the total population of the state. Thirty-nine percent of all native Hawaiian adult deaths are due to suicide, and adolescents have a significantly higher attempt rate (12.9 percent) than the total population (9.6 percent).

Equally alarming are figures on incarceration. Native Hawaiian men comprise between 35 and 43 percent of each security class in Hawai'i's prisons. Native Hawaiian women comprise 38 to 50 percent of each class of inmates. Hawaiians are 40 percent of those with felony convictions versus 25 percent for Caucasians. Seventy percent of all native Hawaiian inmates are between the ages of twenty and forty years of age (Inouye and Akaka 2007, 32–33). As Hawai'i's prisons become overcrowded, Hawaiian prisoners are shipped to prisons on the continent, putting two thousand miles of ocean between prisoners, their families, and the 'āina. RaeDeen Keahiolalo-Karasuda recently wrote her Ph.D. dissertation about this incarceration. She includes a story about a Hawaiian graduate student who spoke at a University of Hawai'i symposium of his time as an inmate in a maximum security facility on O'ahu. "The presenter made one simple yet profound comment that will forever be etched in my mind. He told the audience that every night it would take the guards over fifteen minutes to call Hawaiian last names beginning with the letter 'K.' I was struck by his statement, because it made me realize that this represented the roll call of Hawaiians" (Keahiolalo-Karasuda 2008, 1).

Other indicators are as troubling. In a state with such a high cost of living, Hawai'i's indigenous people are in the most trouble economically. The 2006 *Native Hawaiian Data Book* states,

> Statistics from data indexes relating to income, employment, and public assistance show that Native Hawaiians still rank among the highest in negative social indicators. Native Hawaiians are among those with the lowest median incomes, highest unemployment rates, and highest dependence on government assistance programs such as TANF. What is very disturbing is that Hawaiians represent the highest percentage of homeless in Hawaii. (State of Hawai'i Department of Business 2006, 113)

Poverty statistics show 14 percent of native Hawaiian families and 16 percent of individuals at or below the poverty line. Thirty-two percent of individuals served by Temporary Assistance for Needy Families (TANF)/Temporary Assistance for Other Needy Families (TANOF) programs are native Hawaiian, compared to 15 percent for Caucasians (State of Hawai'i Department of Business 2006, 114–118).

All of this has contributed to an out-migration of native Hawaiians at the same time the overall population of the state is growing. The census category of native Hawaiian and other Pacific Islanders (which is largely Hawaiians) showed a decrease from 23.4 percent of the state's total population in 2000 to 21.4 percent in 2006 (*Honolulu Advertiser* Staff 2007). Eugene Tian, an economist for the state, called the 1.3 percent decrease from 2000 to 2004 significant, so this 2 percent decrease is even more worrisome. Birth and death rates have held fairly consistent for Kanaka Maoli, so Tian states that "from the data, it looks like they're migrating out of state" (Pang 2005). In comparison, the number of haoles is growing at about the same rate Hawai'i is losing Hawaiians. In 2000, haoles made up 40.3 percent of the population, and in 2006 this was up to 42.6 percent (*Honolulu Advertiser* Staff 2007).

A 2005 study comparing native Hawaiian populations in Hawai'i and on the continent, not surprisingly, found those on the continent to have a better socioeconomic status (Malone and Shoda-Sutherland 2005). According to the study, those in Hawai'i are more likely to be unemployed, have a lower per capita income, live in poverty (especially children), and are less likely to be enrolled in higher education or have a college degree. The authors conclude that "the persistent pressures that may motivate Native Hawaiians to move to the continental United States may someday tip the scales such that the majority of *kānaka maoli* will live outside the Hawaiian Islands and away from the *'āina* that has historically been a cornerstone in the foundation of Native Hawaiian well-being" (Malone and Shoda-Sutherland 2005, 9).

Opponents of Hawaiian entitlements mostly ignore these figures. When that does not work, they dismiss them or weakly dispute them, saying Hawaiians are not real victims. Typical is the argument that frames African Americans, and occasionally Native Americans, as the nation's only true victims. A letter to the editor regarding Hawaiian claims states, "Well, why doesn't each of these people who truly feels oppressed go talk to some African-American families who have roots in the slave movement or maybe even Native Americans from the Cherokee Indian Tribe who had a family in the Trail of Tears?" (Eugene 2005).

Less typical are attempts to directly dispute the socioeconomic data, but they do exist. Ken Conklin, an avid opponent of native rights, is forthright in his disbelief of claims "that ethnic Hawaiians have the worst statistics for income, education, unemployment, drug abuse, and diseases" (Conklin 2006). He finds "such victimhood claims are mostly bogus because they ignore that ethnic Hawaiians are 13 years younger on average than other groups, and about 3/4 of 'Native Hawaiian' victims each have more than 3/4 of their ancestry from Asia, Europe, and America" (Conklin 2006). It is unclear what the point of the claim about age is supposed to mean, except that it does underscore truncated life expectancy for Hawaiians. (Geographer Ruth Wilson Gilmore identifies structural conditions that lead to "pre-mature death" as the essence of institutional racism.)[6] The claim that native Hawaiians are not Hawaiian because of their mixed ancestry is common. It is part of the historical colonial move to statistically eliminate native peoples through blood quantum requirements. Kanaka Maoli, however, insist on genealogy as the basis of their community, so that anyone with a Hawaiian ancestor is Hawaiian.

It is not coincidental that Conklin, Rice, Burgess, and others all use the language of "victims" and "victimhood" in their attacks on native entitlements. Political scientist Alyson Cole traces a rise in "anti-victimist" discourse in the United States since the early 1990s. She finds those leading the charge on the political right attack "self-anointed phony" victims and claim to know, or be, the "true victims." At this point in this chapter, this should sound familiar. Cole writes, "Anti-victimism castigates victims for shamelessly using their disadvantage, misfortune, or personal failures to plunder the public coffers" (Cole 2007, 169), thereby victimizing "regular" Americans. Or, in its pernicious island version, victimizing all those residents who love Hawai'i, regardless of their race.

"Anti-victimism . . . categorically denies systemic inequalities and delegitimizes collective action. It is unremittingly privatizing and therapeutic, for it displaces or translates issues of institutional power and social inequality into matters of character" (Cole 2007, 19). We certainly see this in Harold Rice's earlier statement about Hawaiians "stepping over the line." They were trying to "take advantage" of state resources rather than taking care of themselves. Not only is their claim for "racial preferences" unconstitutional, worse, it is un-Hawaiian because it "violates the law of the aloha spirit." How better to attack Kanaka Maoli character? There is certainly no room here for discussions of systemic inequality or institutional power.

## Conclusion

So, is haole victimized? Having analyzed the data, it is clear the answer is no. As we have seen, there is little evidence supporting widespread physical violence against haoles, and the claims of anti-haole legal discrimination crumble under scrutiny. Socioeconomic data reveal that it is Kanaka Maoli who are suffering most in the islands. Programs and entitlements benefiting Kanaka Maoli are small steps toward reconciliation for colonization, an illegal overthrow, and annexation. The use of civil rights laws—intended to end centuries of institutionalized white supremacy—to attack native Hawaiian entitlements is absurdly unjust.

That does not mean that haoles do not sometimes still get harassed for being haole, and while that is absolutely wrong, it does not constitute institutional oppression. If that harassment is increasing, it is worth asking what socioeconomic and political factors might be fueling it. An analysis of the structural violence associated with colonization provides one productive avenue for contextualizing and analyzing anger toward haoles. Equally important to keep in mind is that representing all efforts to build native Hawaiian and local culture as "anti-haole" grossly oversimplifies the matter. Often these efforts decenter haole by going about the work of cultural transformation in local and Hawaiian communities, giving haole neither power nor attention. Haoles tend to think everything is about us. It is not.

The notion that haoles could somehow be victims is ridiculous once put in context. In fact, Hawaiʻi's colonial history has molded the islands into a place that institutionally works well for haoles. That is demonstrated in the socioeconomic data, and yet there are haoles who would turn this history upside down in order to claim victimization and destroy the very institutions and programs enabling Hawaiians to recuperate from centuries of colonial violence. Is it any wonder, then, that there are those who want to claim the islands as a place for "locals only" or those with "koko"? The question for haoles is, What is a *just* response?

# CONCLUSION

It has been over thirty years since I was literally pushed into recognizing myself as haole in that cafeteria line at Kōloa Elementary. Thankfully, I now understand much more about the remark "fucking haole" and about the ways haole has been produced as part of the colonization of Hawai'i. Yet one of the things about writing a book is that it forces you to realize how much you do not know about the topic. No matter how hard you try, there are some things you can never know since we each can only ever have partial knowledge, and since knowledge is so dynamic. It is humbling—perhaps a good antidote for haole hubris. There is much more to be said, and there will be those who disagree with what I have said. Hopefully this book enlivens discussion of haole, colonization, and racial politics in the islands and moves it forward.

Looking at haole through historical, relational, performative, discursive, and material lenses makes it clear that haole did not just naturally come to be in Hawai'i and to dominate political and economic power. Instead, haole gained power in the century after Captain Cook's landing by radically transforming the islands and wresting power from Kanaka Maoli who were suffering devastating losses from haole diseases. A haole oligarchy was then built on the backs of immigrant labor who also built local culture. Colonization worked, and continues to work, through science, religion, law, politics, capitalism, education, language, and print media to mold Hawai'i to fit Western desires. This process of transformation has been written into the dominant history of the islands as "progress," as nonviolent development, and as American manifest destiny culminating in annexation. New scholarship, much of which I have referenced, is challenging this narrative, especially through the investigation of Hawaiian-language primary sources. As more of this research is undertaken, the history of the islands will be rewritten. Significantly,

Kanaka Maoli and local resistance to, and challenges of, haole dominance will receive their due analysis, no longer obscured or dismissed as
inconsequential. It is an exciting time to be studying Hawai'i's history
and thinking about island politics.

As a social construction continually worked on by processes of
racialization that affect everyone in Hawai'i, haole can be thought of as
one of many forms of whiteness. As a name given to white people in the
United States by racialized others, it is similar to honky or cracker. As
a colonial form of American whiteness, haole is similar to gringo. As a
Pacific form of imperial whiteness, it is similar to Pākehā ("whiteness"
in Aotearoa). It is well worth thinking about the similarities and differences between haole and other forms of whiteness. Understanding haole
in historical context, it is useful to think about it as a counternarrative of
whiteness developed by native Hawaiian and local communities. Local
and native constructions of haole are forms of resistance articulated by
those subjugated by haole dominance.

Throughout the book I have examined common haole responses to
being marked as haole. I have challenged the haole tendency to try to
slide out of haole by representing oneself as kama'āina, hapa, Hawaiian
at heart, or even Hawaiian. It is disrespectful to try to escape the historical weight of haole by appropriating Kanaka Maoli culture. I have
argued that loudly protesting the use of the word "haole" is about as
haole as it gets. I have contested the growing discourse among haoles of
haole victimization, especially through the portrayal of native Hawaiians as victimizers. By making ourselves victims, haoles can neatly duck
out of our responsibility for the consequences of colonialism.

So you might be asking yourself at this point, What is it that haoles are supposed to do? For those of us who identify as haole, are we to
go around racked with guilt? Are we to leave Hawai'i? Feeling guilty
at least indicates that we have developed some understanding of the
situation, but it is not a good place to stop, as it helps no one. Leaving
is certainly an option, but there are practical problems. Unless you are
indigenous to some other place on the planet, you will always be on
colonized ground. This is certainly true on the continent, where brutal
colonial histories are buried just a little bit deeper in time and where
there is a relatively smaller native population entreating us to remember. Also, it is hard to see how leaving, unless done en masse, would
really have a material impact.

Perhaps this is the wrong way to think about it. Focusing on questions of guilt and staying or leaving assumes haole as a natural category and misses the performative aspects of haole. Instead of trying to escape the colonial weight of haole, perhaps we can transform haole by directly addressing it. If haole has been constructed in different ways, at different times, by different groups, how might we now produce haole in new ways? Perhaps the question we should be asking is, How can we inhabit haole differently? I do not have The Answer, but I believe there are many if we address the question with honesty, respect, humility, and imagination.

It is important to think about attitudes and actions. It is not just white people who act haole, as whiteness seeps across racial lines. As Davianna McGregor has suggested, acting haole is expecting Hawai'i to assimilate to America (and here she means dominant white U.S. culture). The more one acts out these attitudes of superiority and insensitivity, the more one slides to the far end of the Turnbull continuum from "haole" to "fucking haole." Consciously working against that slide must therefore include assimilating oneself to local and Hawaiian cultures— learning, supporting, and participating in island life *without* pretending to be Hawaiian.

One place to start is by educating ourselves about Hawai'i's history, as well as more generally about white supremacy. Listening and reflecting are crucial to that process. A second step might include recognizing that each of us has multiple identities, that none of us is simply haole, Hawaiian, or local. Many of us claim multiple racial affiliations, in addition to an unending and always shifting host of other identities, including gender, sexuality, ability, class, age, nationality, region, and religion. Since one is never simply haole, what tools can haoles find in our complex identities to help build understandings, alliances, and coalitions without denying our haoleness? Action founded on shared political commitment, on coalition across difference, that does not flatten difference, might be most effective—at least more so than action taken from a place of obligation, guilt, charity, or some form of self-actualization.

It is up to each of us who recognize ourselves as haole to write the future of haole. How will we respond to local efforts to build local culture and reclaim HCE as a legitimate language? How will we respond to representations of Hawai'i as a racial paradise that obscure inequality and the legacies of colonial violence? How will we respond to representations of island culture as overwhelmingly anti-haole? How will we respond to the militarization and commercialization of the islands—

whose homeland are we "securing," whose culture are we selling? How will we respond to Kanaka Maoli efforts at recuperating their culture and their lāhui (nation, people)? How will we respond to the escalating attacks against Hawaiian entitlements and programs? The way we answer these questions, the actions we take individually and collectively, will determine the next chapter of haoles in Hawai'i.

# Notes

## Introduction

1. Local people also refer to the U.S. continent as the "mainland," but there is a political move against that label as it assumes a marginal position for the islands. Hawaiian nationals also refer to the U.S. continent as "America" in order to underscore their claims that Hawai'i is not legally part of the United States. Of course, those from Central and South America, as well as Canada, resist the conflation of "America" with the United States.

2. I put "states" in quotes to highlight the contested nature of Hawai'i's statehood.

3. State and federal bureaucracies make distinctions based on blood quantum between "native Hawaiian" (50 percent native Hawaiian blood or more) and "Hawaiian" (less than 50 percent), but I do not. Some in the Hawaiian community also use the term Kanaka 'Ōiwi, which literally means "bone people," or Hawaiian by ancestry.

4. These numbers are derived from the 2000 census and available from the Hawai'i State Data Book: http://hawaii.gov/dbedt/info/economic/databook/.

5. For more on how the tourist industry represents Hawai'i as an exotic paradise, see Trask 1999.

6. Some good places to start investigating postcolonial theory include Mohanty 2003; McClintock, Mufti, and Shohat 1997; Lewis and Mills 2003.

7. Some places to start exploring critical whiteness studies include Fine 1997, Delgado and Stefancic 1999, Hill 1997, Frankenberg 1997, Haney-López 1996.

8. Some would argue that these powerful locals have become so haolified that they no longer represent Hawaiian/local culture or values. Further, there is a strong critique suggesting that locals need to take responsibility for their complicity with, and sometimes active participation in, the colonization of Hawai'i and the oppression of native Hawaiians (Fujikane 2000, 2004; Trask 2000; Rosa 2000).

## Chapter 1
### "Haole Go Home": Isn't Hawai'i Part of the U.S.?

1. This new scholarship includes Silva 2004, Kame'eleihiwa 1992, Osorio 2002, McGregor 2007, Meyer 2008, Kauanui 2008.

2. Jonathan K. Osorio writes eloquently about this idea of the "dismemberment" of the Hawaiian people and nation (2002).

3. For more on the transformation from traditional to Western law, see Merry 2000.

4. For more on the Māhele, see Kame'eleihiwa 1992; Osorio 2002, 44; Kent 1989, 32.

5. The first sugar plantation was opened in Kōloa and was still in operation in the 1970s when I attended Kōloa Elementary School. The school bus drove out on a cane road to pick up and drop off many of my local classmates whose families worked at the plantation.

6. For a detailed discussion of these debates, see Bell 1984.

7. In the first decades after Cook's arrival Hawai'i was a stopping place for fur traders from the United States and England on their way to China (Kent 1983, 14).

8. Importantly, Noenoe Silva points out significant problems with the published versions of Kamakau's writings in which passages were deleted and reordered in order to make the text fit Western standards of "history" (Silva 2004, 16–23).

9. Much excellent scholarship has focused on the immigration of laborers and the plantation system, and I will return to some of it in my discussion of local identity in chapter 2. See, for example, Takaki 1983, Okihiro 1991, Tamura 1993.

10. See chapter 2 of *Aloha Betrayed* (Silva 2004, 45–86).

11. See chapter 5 of *Aloha Betrayed* (Silva 2004, 164–203).

12. For more on militarism in Hawai'i, see Kajihiro 2002, Ferguson and Turnbull 1999, Trask 2002b, Churchill and Venne 2004. For more on tourism in Hawai'i, see Halualani 2002, Bacchilega 2007, Trask 1999, Desmond 2001.

## Chapter 2
### "No Ack!": What Is Haole, Anyway?

1. *Aloha Betrayed* is the title of Noenoe K. Silva's book about Hawaiian resistance to the overthrow (2004).

2. This can be contrasted with postcolonial theory's intense attention to all forms of resistance by the colonized including evasion, mimicry, and subversion.

3. For more on representations of the queen, see the final chapter in Silva's book and Lydia Kualapai's article (Silva 2004, Kualapai 2005).

4. The military question was not so much about the military *use* of territories or harbors, which U.S. foreign policy makes clear does not require U.S. soil/water. In fact, the United States had already secured use of Pearl Harbor through the Reciprocity Treaty. At issue was the threat to such control posed by other nations with an interest in the islands, particularly Britain, France, and Japan. This threat then built the imperial preference for uncontested ownership.

5. Amongst the evidence Bell presents is this statement by a Missouri congressman: "How can we endure our shame when a Chinese senator from Hawaii, with his pig-tail hanging down his back, with his pagan joss in hand, shall rise from his curule chair and in pidgin English proceed to chop logic with George Frisbie Hoar or Henry Cabot Lodge?" (Bell 1984, 33).

6. In observing how many white people claim a Cherokee princess as a distant relative, one Native American ironically noted, "Like the mythological Christmas fruitcake, there was only one, but she got around" (Garroutte 2003, 91).

7. This is the title of a good short documentary on the subject (Macy and Hart 1995).

8. This is similar to my childhood response of insisting I was Greek, Mexican, Swiss-German, and Swedish.

9. There is, for example, no argument about whether people should keep peppering their speech with the more benign puka (hole) or pau (finished).

10. For more on the Lono controversy, see Borofsky, Hereniko, and Smith in Borofsky 2000; also Merry 2000, 332n9.

11. For more on the plantation system, see Takaki 1983, Fuchs 1961, Kent 1983.

12. For more on Hawai'i's interracial labor unions, see Takaki 1983, Jung 2003.

13. In the 1930s a study showed that 80 percent of Mānoa property was owned by haoles (Rosa 2000, 98).

14. Phyllis Turnbull, e-mail message to author, December 6, 2004.

## Chapter 3
### "Eh, Haole": Is 'Haole' a Derogatory Word?

1. For more of my analysis of this incident, see Rohrer 1997.

2. For more on the Massie affair, see Rosa 2000, Stannard 2005.

3. Anecdotal evidence for this comes from my experience writing my dissertation while living on the continent. Unless I was explicit about my

politics, white people frequently heard my topic, haoles in Hawai'i, as a sign of racial allegiance. More than once I had someone launch into a story about some "anti-haole" incident he/she, a friend, or a family member experienced while on vacation in the islands.

## Chapter 4
## "Locals Only" and "Got Koko?": Is Haole Victimized?

1. Local literature is an excellent source for exploration of the construction of local identity in public schools. Authors including Lois Ann Yamanaka, R. Zamora Linmark, and many of those publishing with Bamboo Ridge provide insight.

2. For more on Kingdom of Hawai'i crown lands, see Van Dyke 2008.

3. Kyle Kajihiro, e-mail communication with author regarding the amount of military lands that are "ceded" lands, April 4, 2008.

4. Judy Roher, "Got Race? The Production of Haole and the Distortion of Indigeneity in the *Rice* Decision," *The Contemporary Pacific* 18(1): 1–31.

5. A law banning Hawaiian language in public schools was passed in 1896 by the Republic of Hawai'i and was not revoked until 1986 (Churchill and Venne 2004, 605).

6. See Gilmore 2002.

# Hawaiian-Language Glossary

**Note:** The translations given here are abbreviations from the Pukui-Elbert Hawaiian-language dictionary focused on usage in this book (Pukui and Elbert 1986).

| | |
|---|---|
| 'āina | land, earth |
| akua | god, goddess, spirit, ghost, devil |
| aloha | love, affection, compassion, mercy, sympathy, pity, kindness, sentiment, grace, charity |
| ali'i | chief, chiefess, officer, ruler |
| hānai | foster child, adopted child; foster, adopted |
| haole | white person, American, Englishman, Caucasian; American, English; formerly, any foreigner; foreign, introduced, of foreign origin, as plants, pigs, chickens [In this book, my usage of "haole" employs native Hawaiian, Hawai'i Creole English, and postmodern meanings. I use it to reference white people, but more broadly, whiteness in Hawai'i, i.e., the power that has accrued through colonization, as well as identity, culture, ideology, and performance.] |
| hapa | portion, fragment, part, fraction, installment; to be partial, less; of mixed blood, person of mixed blood |
| ka 'ōlelo 'ōiwi | the native language of the Kanaka Maoli |
| kalo | taro, a kind of aroid cultivated since ancient times for food, spreading widely from the tropics of the Old World |
| kama'āina | native-born, one born in a place, host |
| Kanaka Maoli | full-blooded Hawaiian person [In this book, I am using a more contemporary definition to include all native Hawaiians, regardless of blood quantum.] |

| | |
|---|---|
| kaona | hidden meaning, as in Hawaiian poetry |
| kapu | taboo, prohibition; forbidden; sacred |
| koko | blood |
| Kū'ē | to oppose, resist, protest |
| kuleana | right, privilege, concern, responsibility |
| kumulipo | origin, genesis, source of life, mystery; name of the Hawaiian creation chant |
| kupuna | grandparent, ancestor, relative or close friend of the grandparent's generation, grandaunt, granduncle |
| lāhui | nation, tribe, people, nationality |
| limu | general name for all kinds of plants living under water |
| lo'i | irrigated terrace, especially for taro |
| Lono | one of the four major gods brought from Kahiki |
| luna | foreman, boss, leader, overseer, supervisor |
| maka'āinana | commoner, populace, people in general; citizen, subject |
| mālama 'āina | to take care of, tend, attend, care for, preserve, protect, beware, save, maintain the land, earth |
| mana | supernatural or divine power |
| mana'o | thought, idea, belief, opinion, theory |
| mele | song, anthem, or chant of any kind (also poetry, per Noenoe Silva) |
| mo'olelo | story, tale, myth, history, tradition, literature, legend |
| 'ohana | family, relative, kin group; related |
| oli | chant that was not danced to |
| pau | finished, ended, through, terminated |
| pono | goodness, uprightness, morality, moral qualities, correct or proper procedure, excellence, well-being, prosperity, welfare, benefit, behalf, equity, sake, true condition or nature |
| puka | hole |

# Bibliography

Adams, Wanda. 1995. Where Did It Come From? *Honolulu Advertiser*, February 5.

Antone, Rod, and Associated Press Staff. 2003. Kamehameha Sued over Its Admissions. *Honolulu Star-Bulletin*, June 26.

Bacchilega, Cristina. 2007. *Legendary Hawai'i and the Politics of Place: Tradition, Translation, and Tourism*. Philadelphia: University of Pennsylvania Press.

Bailey, Beth, and David Farber. 1993. The "Double V" Campaign in World War II Hawaii: African Americans, Racial Ideology, and Federal Power. *Journal of Social History* 26(4): 817–843.

Ballard, Eric, and Cindy Ballard. 2000. As a Haole, Moving Here Proved to Be Eye-Opener. *Honolulu Advertiser*, September 7, 7.

Banner, Gordon. 2004. Missionaries Galore. *MidWeek*, October 6.

Barayuga, Debra. 2005. Waikele Beating Nets 5-Year Term. *Honolulu Star-Bulletin*, December 4.

Basson, Lauren L. 2005. Fit for Annexation but Unfit to Vote? Debating Hawaiian Suffrage Qualifications at the Turn of the Twentieth Century. *Social Science History* 29(4): 575–598.

Bell, Roger. 1984. *Last among Equals: Hawaiian Statehood and American Politics*. Honolulu: University of Hawai'i Press.

Bingham, Hiram. 1969. *A Residence of Twenty-One Years in the Sandwich Islands*. New York: Praeger Publishers. [Original edition published 1849.]

Bishop, Bernice Pauahi. 2008. Bernice Pauahi Bishop's will and codicils. Available from http://www.ksbe.edu/pauahi/will.php [cited September 27, 2008].

Blaisdell, Kekuni. 2003. Presentation to Noenoe Silva's Indigenous Politics graduate class, UH Mānoa, April 1.

Borofsky, Robert. 2000. *Remembrance of Pacific Pasts: An Invitation to Remake History*. Honolulu: University of Hawai'i Press.

Borzych, Todd. 2007. Don't Denigrate. *Honolulu Weekly*, March 28, 1.

Brislin, Richard. 2005. Tone of Voice Can Be as Important as Words Used. *Honolulu Star-Bulletin,* November 28.

Burgess, H. William. 2007a. Aloha for All. Available from http://www.aloha4all.org/home.aspx [cited December 3, 2007].

———. 2007b. Belief in Equal Protection Not Divisive. *Honolulu Advertiser,* September 7.

Carter, Joey. 1990. The White Male: Being Haole in Hawaii. *Ka Leo O Hawaii,* September 5, 6–7.

Case, Suzanne. 2005. Hawaiians, Too, Can Violate Aloha Spirit. *Honolulu Star-Bulletin,* May 8.

Castle, Alfred L. 1981. Advice for Hawaii: The Dole–Burgess Letters. *Hawaiian Journal of History* 15: 24–30.

Chabram-Dernersesian, Angie. 1999. On the Social Construction of Whiteness within Selected Chicana/o Discourses. In *Displacing Whiteness: Essays in Social and Cultural Criticism,* ed. R. Frankenberg. Durham, N.C.: Duke University Press.

Chang, Jeffrey Kin Wah. 1995. Lessons of Tolerance: Ethnicity, the Local and Affirmative Action in Hawaiʻi. Master's thesis, University of California, Los Angeles.

Churchill, Ward, and Sharon H. Venne, eds. 2004. *Islands in Captivity: The International Tribunal on the Rights of Indigenous Hawaiians.* Cambridge, Mass.: South End Press.

Coffman, Tom. 1998. *Nation Within: The Story of America's Annexation of the Nation of Hawaiʻi.* Kaneohe, Hawaiʻi: Epicenter.

Cole, Alyson M. 2007. *The Cult of True Victimhood: From the War on Welfare to the War on Terror.* Stanford, Calif.: Stanford University Press.

Conklin, Ken. 2006. Why All America Should Oppose the Hawaiian Government Reorganization Bill, Also Known as the Akaka Bill, S.3064, S.147, and H.R.309. Available from http://www.angelfire.com/planet/bigfiles40/AkakaNationalSummary.html [cited April 2, 2008].

Daniel, Marcus. 2003. Don't Hijack King's Message. *Honolulu Advertiser,* August 31.

Daysog, Rick. 2003. Tycoons to Share Tab in Kamehameha Suit. *Honolulu Advertiser,* December 3.

Delgado, Richard, and Jean Stefancic. 1999. *Critical Race Theory: The Cutting Edge.* 2nd ed. Philadelphia: Temple University Press.

Desmond, Jane. 2001. *Staging Tourism: Bodies on Display from Waikiki to Sea World.* Chicago: University of Chicago Press.

Dooley, Jim. 2005. Hawaii Man Sentenced to 5 Years for Beating. *Honolulu Advertiser,* December 4.

———. 2007. Hawaii Reported Total of 6 Hate Crimes in 2006. *Honolulu Advertiser,* November 20.

————. 2008. Kamehameha Settled at $7M. *Honolulu Advertiser,* February 8.

Dooley, Jim, and Gordon Y. K. Pang. 2008. Kamehameha Schools Again Being Sued over Admissions Policy. *Honolulu Advertiser,* August 7.

Duncan, Brook. 2004. OK to Be Haole. *MidWeek,* November 3.

Eugene, Joseph. 2005. It All Boils Down to Racist School Policy. *Honolulu Advertiser,* August 19.

Federal Bureau of Investigation (FBI). 2006. Agency Hate Crime Reporting by State, 2006, Table 12. U.S. Department of Justice. http://www.fbi.gov/ucr/hc2006/table12.html.

Ferguson, Kathy E., and Phyllis Turnbull. 1999. *Oh, Say, Can You See? The Semiotics of the Military in Hawai'i,* Minneapolis: University of Minnesota Press.

Ferrar, Derek. 2008. OHA Prevails in Suit against Hawaiian Benefits. Press release dated April 16, 2007. Available from http://www.oha.org [cited March 30, 2008].

Fine, Michelle. 1997. *Off White: Readings on Race, Power, and Society.* New York: Routledge.

Frankenberg, Ruth. 1996. "When We Are Capable of Stopping, We Begin to See": Being White, Seeing Whiteness. In *Names We Call Home: Autobiography on Racial Identity,* ed. B. W. Thompson and S. Tyagi. New York: Routledge.

————. 1997. *Displacing Whiteness: Essays in Social and Cultural Criticism.* Durham, N.C.: Duke University Press.

Fuchs, Lawrence H. 1961. *Hawaii Pono: A Social History.* San Diego: Harcourt Brace Jovanovich.

Fujikane, Candace. 2000. Asian Settler Colonization of Hawai'i. *Amerasia Journal* 26(2): xv–xxii.

————. 2004. Foregrounding Native Nationalisms: A Critique of Anti-Nationalist Sentiment in Asian American Studies. Honolulu: University of Hawai'i. Presentation at UH Mānoa, March 3, 2004, as part of the Office of Women's Research Brown Bag lunch series.

Gallagher, Charles A. 1997. White Racial Formation: Into the Twenty-First Century. In *Critical White Studies: Looking behind the Mirror,* ed. R. Delgado and J. Stefancic. Philadelphia: Temple University Press.

Galtung, Johan. 1969. Violence, Peace and Peace Research. *Journal of Peace Research* 6(3): 167–191.

————. 1990. Cultural Violence. *Journal of Peace Research* 27(2): 291–305.

Garroutte, Eva Marie. 2003. *Real Indians: Identity and the Survival of Native America.* Berkeley: University of California Press.

Gilmore, Ruth Wilson. 2002. Fatal Couplings of Power and Difference: Notes on Racism and Geography. *The Professional Geographer* 54(1): 15–24.

114                                    BIBLIOGRAPHY

Gima, Craig. 1999. "Kill Haole Day" Linked to Hate-Crime Bill. *Honolulu Star-Bulletin*, March 24, 4.
Glenn, Evelyn Nakano. 2002. *Unequal Freedom: How Race and Gender Shaped American Citizenship and Labor.* Cambridge, Mass.: Harvard University Press.
Grant, Glen. 1978. Race Relations in the Hawaiian School: The *Haole* Newcomer. In *Kodomo No Tame Ni (For the Sake of the Children): The Japanese American Experience in Hawai'i,* ed. D. M. Ogawa. Honolulu: University of Hawai'i Press.
Grant, Glen, and Dennis M. Ogawa. 1993. Living Proof: Is Hawaii the Answer? *The Annals of the American Academy* 530: 137–154.
Grimshaw, Patricia. 1985. New England Missionary Wives, Hawaiian Women, and "The Cult of True Womanhood." *The Hawaiian Journal of History* 19: 71–100.
———. 1989. *Paths of Duty: American Missionary Wives in Nineteenth-Century Hawaii.* Honolulu: University of Hawai'i Press.
Haas, Michael. 1992. *Institutional Racism: The Case of Hawai'i.* Westport, Conn.: Praeger.
Haire, Chris. 2007. Eh, Haole: Hawaiian Studies Professor Kanalu Young Discusses the Controversial Word for White People. *Honolulu Weekly,* August 8–14, 1.
Hall, Lisa Kahaleole. 2005. "Hawaiian at Heart" and Other Fictions. *The Contemporary Pacific* 17(2): 404–413.
Halualani, Rona Tamiko. 2002. *In the Name of Hawaiians: Native Identities & Cultural Politics.* Minneapolis: University of Minnesota Press.
Haney-López, Ian. 1996. *White by Law: The Legal Construction of Race, Critical America.* New York: New York University Press.
Harris, Cheryl I. 1993. Whiteness as Property. *Harvard Law Review* 106: 1707–1791.
Herman, R. Douglas K. 1995. Kalai'aina—Carving the Land: Geography, Desire and the Possession in the Hawaiian Islands. Ph.D. dissertation, University of Hawai'i, Mānoa.
Hill, Mike. 1997. *Whiteness: A Critical Reader.* New York: New York University Press.
*Honolulu Advertiser* Staff. 2007. New Census Figures Show Hawaii Population Shifting. *Honolulu Advertiser,* August 8.
*Honolulu Star-Bulletin* Editorial Staff. 2007. Waikele Beating Does Not Meet Hate-Crime Standard. *Honolulu Star-Bulletin,* February 28.
*Honolulu Star-Bulletin* Staff & Associated Press. 2008. Kamehameha Schools Face Another Challenge to Admissions. *Honolulu Star-Bulletin,* August 6.
Jeong, David. 2006. Diversity Makes Isles Perfect Place to Live. *Honolulu Advertiser,* February 18, 1.

Judd, Laura Fish. 1961. Leaves from a Missionary's Diary. In *A Hawaiian Reader,* ed. A. G. Day and C. Stroven. New York: Popular Library.

Jung, Moon-Kie. 2003. Interracialism: The Ideological Transformation of Hawaii's Working Class. *American Sociological Review* 68(3): 373–400.

*Ka Leo O Hawaii* Editors. Trask: Racist or Righteous? 1990. Letters to the editor, *Ka Leo O Hawaii,* September 26, 4.

Kajihiro, Kyle. 2002. Militarizing Hawai'i: Occupation, Accommodation and Resistance. Unpublished paper. American Friends Service Committee, Honolulu.

———. 2007. A Brief Overview of Militarization and Resistance in Hawai'i. Unpublished paper. DMZ-Hawai'i/Aloha 'Aina, Honolulu.

Kamakau, Samuel M. 1992. *Ruling Chiefs of Hawaii.* Rev. ed. Honolulu: Kamehameha Schools Press. [Original edition published 1961.]

Kame'eleihiwa, Lilikalā. 1992. *Native Land and Foreign Desires.* Honolulu: Bishop Museum Press.

Kame'eleihiwa, Lilikalā, and Gayatri Chakravorty Spivak. 2003. Two Worlds Meeting: Lilikala Kame'eleihiwa and Gayatri Chakravorty Spivak—Conversations on Indigenous Issues and Settler Viewpoints. Presentation at the Center for Hawaiian Studies, April 9, Honolulu.

Kamehameha Schools Board of Trustees. 2008. KS Sues John Doe for Breach of Contract; Receives Demand Letter Threatening New Lawsuit from Eric Grant. Available from www.ksbe.edu [cited September 2, 2008].

Kana'iapuni, S. K., N. Malone, and K. Ishibashi. 2005. *Ka Huaka'i: 2005 Native Hawaiian Educational Assessment.* Honolulu: Kamehameha Schools, Pauahi Publications.

Kasindorf, Martin. 2007. Racial Tensions Are Simmering in Hawaii's Melting Pot. *USA Today,* March 6.

Kauanui, J. Kēhaulani. 1999. "For Get" Hawaiian Entitlement: Configurations of Land, "Blood," and Americanization in the Hawaiian Homes Commission Act of 1921. *Social Text* 59 (Summer): 123–144.

———. 2000. Rehabilitating the Native: Hawaiian Blood Quantum and the Politics of Race, Citizenship, and Entitlement. Ph.D. dissertation, University of California, Santa Cruz.

———. 2002. The Politics of Blood and Sovereignty in *Rice v. Cayetano.* *PoLAR* 25(1): 110–128.

———. 2008. Hawaiian Blood: Colonialism and the Politics of Sovereignty and Indigeneity. Durham, N.C.: Duke University Press.

Keahiolalo-Karasuda, RaeDeen. 2008. The Colonial Carceral and Prison Politics in Hawai'i. Ph.D. dissertation, University of Hawai'i.

Kent, Noel J. 1983. *Hawaii, Islands under the Influence.* New York: Monthly Review Press.

Kirkpatrick, John. 1987. Ethnic Antagonism and Innovation in Hawaii. In *Ethnic Conflict: International Perspectives,* ed. J. Boucher, D. Landis, and K. A. Clark. Newbury Park, Calif.: Sage Publications.

KITV. 2007. Attorney Solicits Plaintiffs for Kamehameha Schools Lawsuit. Available at http://www.kitv.com/education/13370001/detail.html [cited May 22, 2007].

Kraemer, Kelly Rae. 2000. Shall We Overcome? Politics of Allies in the Hawaiian Sovereignty, Civil Rights, and Women's Movements. Ph.D. dissertation, University of Hawai'i, Mānoa.

Kreifels, Susan. 1999a. Is Trouble Brewing? *Honolulu Star-Bulletin,* April 23.

———. 1999b. State's History Nurtures Ethnic Animosity: The Way People Treated Each Other through the Years Is Not Forgotten. *Honolulu Star-Bulletin,* April 23.

Kualapai, Lydia K. 2001. Cast in Print: The Nineteenth-Century Hawaiian Imaginary. Ph.D. dissertation, University of Nebraska.

———. 2005. The Queen Writes Back: Lili'uokalani's Hawaii's Story by Hawaii's Queen. *Studies in American Indian Literatures* 17(2): 32–62.

Kubo, Louise M. 1997. Reading and Writing Local: A Politics of Community. Ph.D. dissertation, University of Hawai'i, Mānoa.

Lee, Bradford. 2003. Hawaiian Geopolitics. *Honolulu Weekly,* vol. 13, no. 8 (February 19–25), 3.

Lewis, Reina, and Sara Mills. 2003. *Feminist Postcolonial Theory: A Reader.* Edinburgh: Edinburgh University Press.

Lili'uokalani. 1964. *Hawaii's Story by Hawaii's Queen.* Rutland, Vt.: Charles E. Tuttle Company.

Lipsitz, George. 2006. *The Possessive Investment in Whiteness: How White People Profit from Identity Politics.* Rev. ed. Philadelphia: Temple University Press.

Love, Eric Tyrone Lowery. 1997. Race over Empire: Racism and United States Imperialism, 1865–1900. Ph.D. dissertation, Princeton University.

Macy, Terry, and Daniel Hart, directors. 1995. *White Shamans, Plastic Medicine Men.* DVD. Native Voices Public Television.

Malone, Nolan J., and Carrie Shoda-Sutherland. 2005. *Kau Li'ili'i: Characteristics of Native Hawaiians in Hawai'i and the Continental United States.* Honolulu: Kamehameha Schools–PASE.

Matsunaga, Mark. 1995. "Haole" Ruled OK, by Itself: Embellishment Can Make It Racial Slur. *Honolulu Advertiser,* February 10, 3.

McClintock, Anne, Aamir Mufti, and Ella Shohat. 1997. *Dangerous Liaisons: Gender, Nation, and Postcolonial Perspectives.* Minneapolis: University of Minnesota Press.

McGregor, Davianna Pōmaika'i. 1989. Ho'omauke Ea O Ka Lahui Hawai'i: The Perpetuation of the Hawaiian People. In *Ethnicity and Nation-Building in the Pacific*, ed. M. C. Howard. Tokyo: The United Nations University.

———. 2007. *Nā Kua'āina: Living Hawaiian Culture*. Honolulu: University of Hawai'i Press.

Memminger, Charles. 2006. "Keel Haole" Idea Is Left for Dead. *Honolulu Star-Bulletin*, August 6.

Merry, Sally Engle. 2000. *Colonizing Hawai'i: The Cultural Power of Law*. Princeton, N.J.: Princeton University Press.

Merry, Sally Engle, and Donald Brenneis, eds. 2003. *Law & Empire in the Pacific: Fiji and Hawai'i*, ed. R. M. Leventhal. School of American Research Advanced Seminar Series. Santa Fe, N.M.: School of American Research Press.

Meyer, Manulani Aluli. 2008. *Hawaiian Knowing: Old Ways for Seeing a New World*. Kihei, Hawai'i: Koa Books.

Milner, Neal, and Jon Goldberg-Hiller. 2002. Post-Civil Rights Context and Special Rights Claims: Native Hawaiian Autonomy, U.S. Law, and International Politics. Paper presented at the Law and Society Annual Meeting, Vancouver.

Mohanty, Chandra Talpade. 2003. *Feminism without Borders: Decolonizing Theory, Practicing Solidarity*. Durham, N.C.: Duke University Press.

Moon, Jade. 2004. The H Word Is Harmless in Hawaii. *MidWeek*, September 8, 1.

Nordyke, Eleanor C. 1989. *The Peopling of Hawai'i*. Honolulu: University of Hawai'i Press.

O'Connor, Dennis, Jr. 2004. What's in a Name? *MidWeek*, September 22.

Odo, Franklin. 2004. *No Sword to Bury: Japanese Americans in Hawai'i during World War II*. Philadelphia: Temple University Press.

OHA Public Information Office. 2007. Kau Inoa Presses Ahead Despite Possible Threat of Legal Attack, September 4. Available from http://www.oha.org [cited March 30, 2008].

Ohnuma, Keiko. 2002. Local Haole—Contradiction in Terms? The Dilemma of Being White, Born and Raised in Hawai'i. *Cultural Values* 6(3): 273–285.

Okamura, Jonathan. 1998. The Illusion of Paradise: Privileging Multiculturalism in Hawai'i. In *Making Majorities: Constituting the Nation in Japan, Korea, China, Malaysia, Fiji, Turkey and the United States*, ed. D. C. Gladney. Stanford, Calif.: Stanford University Press.

Okihiro, Gary Y. 1991. *Cane Fires: The Anti-Japanese Movement in Hawaii, 1865–1945*. Philadelphia: Temple University Press.

Osorio, Jonathan Kay Kamakawiwoʻole. 2002. *Dismembering Lāhui: A History of the Hawaiian Nation to 1887*. Honolulu: University of Hawaiʻi Press.

Pang, Gordon Y. K. 2005. Native Hawaiian Census Numbers Down. *Honolulu Advertiser*, August 12.

————. 2007. Road Rage Blamed in Waikele Beatings. *Honolulu Advertiser*, February 24.

Perrone, Paul. 2002–2005. *Hate Crimes in Hawaii*. State of Hawaiʻi Department of the Attorney General, Crime Prevention & Justice Assistance Division. Available from http://hawaii.gov/ag/cpja [cited April 16, 2008].

Pierce, Lori. 2004. "The Whites Have Created Modern Honolulu": Ethnicity, Racial Stratification, and the Discourse of Aloha. In *Racial Thinking in the United States: Uncompleted Independence*, ed. P. Spickard and G. R. Daniel. Notre Dame, Ind.: University of Notre Dame Press.

Pukui, Mary Kawena, and Samuel H. Elbert. 1986. *Hawaiian Dictionary: Hawaiian-English, English-Hawaiian*. Rev. ed. Honolulu: University of Hawaiʻi Press.

Rees, Robert M. 2003. Hawaiian History Can't Be Reduced to Race. *Honolulu Advertiser*, August 31.

Rohrer, Judy. 1997. Haole Girl: Identity and White Privilege in Hawaiʻi. *Social Process in Hawaiʻi* 38: 140–161.

————. 2006. Got Race? The Production of Haole and the Distortion of Indigeneity in the *Rice* Decision. *The Contemporary Pacific* 18(1): 1–31.

Rosa, John P. 2000. Local Story: The Massie Case Narrative and the Cultural Production of Local Identity in Hawaiʻi. *Amerasia Journal* 26(2): 93–115.

Rosen, David R. 2007. Let High Court Hear Admissions Issue. *Honolulu Advertiser*, May 27.

Sanburn, Curt. 1998. Growing up Haole: A Reflection on Race in Hawaiʻi from ʻIolani to Island Politics. *Honolulu Weekly*, May 20, 6.

Saranillio, Dean. 2008. Seeing Hawaiʻi Statehood: Cultural Politics at the Intersections of Race and Indigeneity. Paper presented at the American Studies Association Annual Conference, Albuquerque, N.M.

Silva, Noenoe K. 2004. *Aloha Betrayed: Native Hawaiian Resistance to American Colonialism*. Durham, N.C.: Duke University Press.

Simonson, Douglas. 1981. *Pidgin to Da Max*. Honolulu: Peppovision.

Smith, Linda Tuhiwai. 1999. *Decolonizing Methodologies: Research and Indigenous Peoples*. New York: Zed Books.

Sodetani, Naomi. 2003. Q & A with Waimea Rancher Harold "Freddy" Rice (October 16–31). *Hawaii Island Journal* (online newspaper). Available from http://www.hawaiiislandjournal.com/stories/10b03b.html [cited December 2, 2003].

Stanley, Josh. 2004. Not a Haole. *MidWeek,* October 27.

Stannard, David E. 1989. *Before the Horror: The Population of Hawaii on the Eve of Western Contact.* Honolulu: Social Science Research Institute, University of Hawai'i.

————. 2005. *Honor Killing: How the Infamous "Massie Affair" Transformed Hawai'i.* New York: Viking.

State of Hawai'i Department of Business, Economic Development & Tourism. 2006. *The State of Hawai'i Data Book: A Statistical Abstract.* Available from www.hawaii.gov/dbedt/ [cited April 2, 2008].

SupportKamehameha.org. *About* Doe v. Kamehameha. Cited April 3, 2008.

Takaki, Ronald. 1983. *Pau Hana: Plantation Life and Labor in Hawaii.* Honolulu: University of Hawai'i Press.

Talking *Haole:* No Offense on Its Face. 1995. Editorial, *Honolulu Advertiser,* January 22, B2.

Tamura, Eileen. 1993. *Americanization, Acculturation, and Ethnic Identity: The Nisei Generation in Hawaii.* Urbana: University of Illinois Press.

Trask, Haunani-Kay. 1990. Caucasians Are Haoles. *Ka Leo O Hawaii,* September 19, 5.

————. 1993. *From a Native Daughter: Colonialism & Sovereignty in Hawai'i.* Monroe, Minn.: Common Courage Press.

————. 1999. Lovely Hula Hands: Corporate Tourism and the Prostitution of Hawaiian Culture. In *From a Native Daughter: Colonialism & Sovereignty in Hawai'i.* 2nd ed. Honolulu: University of Hawai'i Press.

————. 2000. Settlers of Color and "Immigrant" Hegemony: "Locals" In Hawai'i. *Amerasia Journal* 26(2): 1–24.

————. 2002a. Pacific Island Women and White Feminism. In *Pacific Diaspora: Island Peoples in the United States and across the Pacific,* ed. P. Spickard, J. L. Rondilla, and D. H. Wright. Honolulu: University of Hawai'i Press.

————. 2002b. Stealing Hawai'i: The War Machine at Work. *Honolulu Weekly,* July 17, 6.

Tumblin, James L. 2004. Tumblin's Thanks. *MidWeek,* October 13.

Turnbull, Phyllis, and Kathy E. Ferguson. 1997. Military Presence/Missionary Past: The Historical Construction of Masculine Order and Feminine Hawai'i. *Social Process in Hawai'i* 38: 96–107.

Twigg-Smith, Thurston. 1998. *Hawaiian Sovereignty: Do the Facts Matter?* Honolulu: Goodale Publishing.

Van Dyke, Jon M. 2008. *Who Owns the Crown Lands of Hawaii?* Honolulu: University of Hawai'i Press.

Viotti, Vicki. 1995. Haole: Is It a Dirty Word? *Honolulu Advertiser,* February 5, F1.

————. 2004. Multicultural or Not, Inequities Continue in Our Society. *Honolulu Advertiser,* October 24.

————. 2005. Teens Take Back School's Image. *Honolulu Advertiser,* February 5.

Whittaker, Elvi. 1986. *The Mainland Haole: The White Experience in Hawaii.* New York: Columbia University Press.

Wilson, Rob. 2000. Exporting Christian Transcendentalism, Importing Hawaiian Sugar: The Trans-Americanization of Hawai'i. *American Literature* 72(3): 521–552.

Wood, Houston. 1999. *Displacing Natives: The Rhetorical Production of Hawai'i.* Lanham, Md.: Rowman & Littlefield Publishers, Inc.

World Travel & Tourism Council. 1999. *WTTC Hawaii Tourism Report 1999.* London: World Travel & Tourism Council.

Young, Lea K. 2006. *2006 Native Hawaiian Data Book,* ed. Office of Board Services. Honolulu: Office of Hawaiian Affairs.

# Index

agriculture: industrial, 15, 25; subsis-
tence, 24
'āina, 14–15, 65
Akaka bill, 87
Aloha Clubs, 45
"Aloha for All," 69
aloha spirit, 63–65, 69, 84, 93, 99
Americanization, 11, 29–30, 40, 41,
79, 94
Anglo, 35, 55, 73, 74. *See also* Caucasian
annexation, 12, 19, 28, 29, 31, 57, 94,
100, 101; Committee of, 39; 1898
Resolution, 86; process and resis-
tance, 21–25; racism and, 39–41;
treaty, 21, 23
Aotearoa, 3, 32, 102
*Arakaki v. Lingle,* 92
Ariyoshi, Gov. George, 67
assimilation, 30, 42. *See also*
Americanization

Big Five, 29
Bingham, Rev. Hiram, 18, 26, 37
Bishop, Princess Bernice Pauahi, 89, 94
Blaisdell, Kekuni, 51
blood quantum, 43, 76, 99, 105n3
Burgess, H. William, 69, 92–93, 99

capitalism, 8, 12, 14, 27, 40, 101; as
means of colonization, 24–26
cartography, 14–15
Caucasian, 9, 35, 47, 53, 59, 61, 72, 74,
94; Portuguese as, 55–56; socioeconomic data about, 96–97. *See also* Anglo

Chabram-Dernersesian, Angie, 35
Christianity, 34, 40; conversion to, 27,
39, 48–49
citizenship, 42–43
civil rights movement, 90
colonization: and capitalism, 24–26;
contemporary, 28–31; defined, 13;
language and communication, 26–28;
law and politics, 18–24; processes
of, 13–16; religion, 16–18; theory of
inevitability, 40; trauma of, 14, 85.
*See also* resistance
colorblind ideology, 3, 8, 9, 46, 53, 69,
78, 87–88
Cook, Capt. James, 3, 5, 8, 17, 33, 35,
52, 101; as "discoverer," 11, 13–15,
36; as a god, 48–49
counterdiscourse (also counternarrative),
22, 34–35, 47–48, 56–57, 74,
77, 102
critical whiteness studies, ix, 7, 105n7
Cruz, Lynette, 23–24

Daniel, Marcus, 90
death, mass, ix, 16–17
Department of Education (DOE), 79, 94
Department of Hawaiian Homelands
(DHHL), 86, 87, 93
depopulation. *See* death, mass
discovery, ix, 11, 13–15, 36
discrimination: alleged against nonlocals,
68, 87, 92–93, 100; against Asians,
41–42; legal protections against, 89.
*See also* racial conflict discourse